BUYING YOUR FIRST HOME

TRIED AND TRUE REAL ESTATE TIPS FOR FINANCE OPTIONS, CLOSING COSTS, AND BUILDING EQUITY TO MASTER THE ART OF HOMEOWNERSHIP

V J DEAN

V J DEAN PUBLICATIONS

CONTENTS

EXCLUSIVE OFFER!

As a small token of my appreciation, here is a Free Gift that will be crucial for your success with this book:

Success Tools for Your New House Hunt: *Free PDF*

This necessary tool is a must as you evaluate and compare amenities when looking at prospective new homes. With it you'll be able to list and detail desired amenities based on your unique desires and needs. It will not only help prioritize what matters most but will also aid in making informed decisions. This focused tool simplifies the comparison of different properties, allowing you to identify the one that best suits your lifestyle and ensures that you can fully enjoy your new home.

CLICK HERE TO GET IT NOW
www.vjdeanpublications.com

INTRODUCTION

When I bought my first house, I thought I understood what it would take to get into my new home, as I had already been in the industry for quite some time, with a bit of experience up my sleeve. However, all those secrets of the trade I had learned over the years didn't change the fact that the journey was daunting and overloaded with tons of information I had learned from many sources. While my real estate background played a crucial role, buying a house now meant that I, as an individual, had to do all the same hard work that all those clients I had worked with had done. They made the choice to buy, looked for the perfect place, jumped through all the hoops of finding a mortgage, dealt with inspectors and reports and repairs, slogged through all the paperwork, made it to the closing table and eventually, walked away with the keys to their new home. So could I.

I had a general idea of what I wanted, but not to the last detail. Maybe you are also in the process of securing your first home, and you have no idea what to look for, what you want, how much you must have, how much space you will need, what to compromise on, and what you must avoid. Have no fear; landing on this comprehensive step-by-step guide is the best decision you made.

There will be choices to be made: do you give up on your ideal location, or house condition, or the size of the home? Will you decide to commute long distances to and from work to get to your new home, or will you buy a home in an easily accessible area that takes a large chunk of your money? These are hard decisions to make. You may be faced with giving up city amenities you want in a prime location for a more spacious home that is far away from those amenities, but is far more affordable. Without the proper guidance, these choices can leave a bitter taste in your mouth. Fortunately, I went through all that turmoil and generously shared my decades of experience in real estate with you in this book so that you do not have to go through all the challenges on your own.

I will tell you all about the upsides and downsides of loans and guide you on what to do regarding down-payment options. I will even share financing options geared specifically for first-time homebuyers that can waive that substantial down payment obstacle or additional insurance costs.

And, what about the current real estate market? As I write, it is marked by a rapid surge in prices and a scarcity of available homes, adds another layer of complexity. Your hard-earned savings may suddenly feel insufficient, and the limited housing options create an unexpected challenge, leaving you uncertain about your next steps. We can agree that navigating the real estate market as a first-time buyer can be a confusing ordeal. With limited experience and market knowledge, you may struggle to identify what truly matters when evaluating a property listing.

Understanding your needs and wants in a home can become baffling. Furthermore, beyond the property itself, the legal aspects of purchasing a home often appear like an intricate web of complexity. The involvement of multiple parties, an avalanche of paperwork, and the coordination of timing can induce stress and confusion, leaving you unsure of where to begin.

If you are tired of going through countless materials with no basic layout structure or actionable steps, Buying Your First Home has come to your rescue. This book is your North Star, guiding you every step of the way. Join me as I unravel the mysteries of first-time homebuying to make this journey less daunting as well as an exciting process. So as we get started, let me just say,

Congratulations! You're on your way to your new home!

1

STARTING YOUR HOMEBUYING JOURNEY

Have you thought about why you want to buy your own house and why now seems like the right time for you? Maybe you are looking for stability and security of being in a place that you can call your own home. Ask yourself if you're happy with your current living situation, and your answer will reveal why you're here or why you want more. Whatever your reason for taking this life-changing step, I can tell you that it will be a fun ride as you learn the process and travel through what it means to own your own home. It can be a rewarding experience; but, it will mean you must have your eyes wide open to pay attention to all the choices and details so that you don't rush into something before you're ready. This chapter looks at the joys that come with homeownership and how you can be prepared for the journey ahead.

BENEFITS OF BUYING A HOME

There are perks to living in a space you own rather than a rented one. While renting can seem more affordable, it might not be the case long-term. A rented place comes with a lot of restrictions, and after all that time and money invested in rent, you end up with nothing. Owning your home is a lifetime investment that you can even pass down to your children or use to secure other investments. Below are some of the many reasons for owning your home, which you can look forward to as you begin this journey.

A Place to Live

Buying a home not only provides you with a place to live but also gives you a sense of stability and security. Rather than moving from place to place as a renter, being a homeowner grounds you in a place where you can build a stable life. If you have children, staying in one school can benefit their performance compared to when they change schools every time their parents move. Therefore, owning a home gives you and your family a place to live and build a life.

It Is More Than an Investment

Your home accrues value over time, and the longer you live in it, the more its value grows. If you were renting, even if you stay a decade in one place, when you leave, you will have accumulated nothing. However, you have a chance to build your equity through mortgage payments. If you live with your family, your home becomes more than a monetary investment because you get to create life-long memories with them.

Save Money With Mortgages

Mortgages act as a forced savings plan because you are paying down something you will eventually own.

Here's an example:

Let's meet Samantha. She used to pay rent every month, feeling like she was just helping her landlord save up. Then, Samantha decided to take the plunge into owning her own home. She talked to lenders and got a loan and bought a house. With her mortgage payments, Samantha wasn't just paying bills; she was building her own financial fortress. Each payment wasn't just money spent - it was an investment in her future. Over time, as she faithfully made those mortgage payments, Samantha saw something incredible happen: her equity grew. Imagine this: a few years later, Samantha's equity had become a significant chunk. When an opportunity arose for a new business venture, Samantha didn't need to look far for funds. She tapped into her home equity, using it as a launchpad for her next big thing.

Later on, when Samantha sold her house to move closer to family, that built-up equity was like a surprise bonus check she received. It was the reward for all those mortgage payments - her own savings fund that had been growing quietly in the background.

That's the beauty of mortgages: they're not just about owning a home. They're a smart way to save and build wealth that can support your dreams along the way.

Stable Housing Costs

Another bonus? Your fixed mortgage rate also means that your principal and interest remain stable for the course of the loan.

Compared to increasing annual rental rates, this predictability and stability can help you to budget your money wisely in the long run.

Community and Neighborhood Involvement

Compared to moving from place to place as a renter, which makes it difficult to belong to one place, being a homeowner makes you a part of a community. You build long-lasting relationships where your roots are grounded. You and your family are also able to participate in community events that grow and improve your neighborhood.

Tax Benefits

Homeownership often comes with tax advantages. You can reduce your tax liability by deducting your mortgage interest and property tax from your taxable income.

Personalized Space

You have the freedom to design or remodel the house you own and personalize it according to your preferences. You can never do anything about the house you rent—not even change the paint color or modernize the kitchen countertops - unless you're willing to change it all back when your lease ends. Personalizing your home makes you feel in your element and gives you a sense of belonging.

Increased Privacy

Owning your space grants you total privacy in your life without a landlord popping in anytime to check on how you are handling their property. No one needs to know what you do with your property or how you live in your home. Additionally, depending on your neighborhood, you can also increase your privacy with high-wall fencing and backyard lattices, or even install an intercom, video doorbell, or other smart home security measures to be in total control of your privacy.

Mortgage-Free Retirement

The earlier you start building the equity of your home, the more you ensure that you will enjoy your golden years of retirement debt-free, having paid up the house. With substantial equity, you can even opt to sell your home and move into a smaller space to enjoy your retirement with more funds.

Build Generational Wealth

In addition to raising your family and creating memories in your home, you can also pass it down from generation to generation and build a life-long legacy. Houses with stable historic ownership are not only sentimental but also have the potential to be more valuable over decades, ensuring that your descendants will be well taken care of.

Potential Side Hustle

If your home has extra space that you do not use, such as an additional bedroom or a basement, you can rent it out to tenants and start a side hustle. The rental income can help offset the mortgage or just come in handy whenever you need cash. If you are up for an income-generating challenge, you can even list your extra space on popular sites like Airbnb to take advantage of nightly accommodation rates, which are much higher than monthly rates. With a good occupancy rate, your home could generate more income that meets your mortgage requirements. You also get to have extra cash.

Asset Protection

Let's look at an example of your home as a protected asset:

Meet Jenna, a savvy investor torn between buying stocks or investing in property. She was intrigued by the stock market's potential but felt a bit uncertain about the intangible nature of stocks.

Looking for something more tangible, Jenna decided to purchase a small condo in a busy city. Unlike stocks floating in the digital realm, Jenna could physically touch and see her property. That sense of tangibility reassured her - it was a real, solid investment.

Months rolled by, and economic times changed. Inflation started creeping up, making the dollar less powerful. Yet, Jenna noticed something interesting: while the dollar's buying power wavered, the value of her new home stood strong. Historically, real estate has this knack for hedging against inflation, and Jenna's property seemed to be doing just that - growing in value while the dollar lost its strength.

Jenna realized that whether she decides to sell her condo down the line or not, it was a smart move. Her real estate investment wasn't just a place to call home; it was a fortress against economic uncertainties with a potential return far beyond what she initially put into it. With her property, she was sitting on something solid and ever-appreciating, unlike the unpredictable ups and downs of the stock market. That's the power of real estate - it's not just a home; it's a growing asset plus a safeguarded asset.

BEING REALISTIC: POTENTIAL BUMPS IN THE ROAD

As much as there are numerous reasons to own a home, it is only fair that you are aware that it is not always going to be a smooth ride. Homeownership comes with its own set of challenges that you must be prepared for so that you are not caught off-guard. As you start this journey, it is most important that you are realistic and weigh your options ahead.

Challenges of Owning a House

High Upfront Costs

We've talked about many benefits to owning your own home, but if you're going to make a good decision, it's wise to think about both sides of the homeownership coin. As I highlighted in the introduction, one of the issues you face in deciding whether or not to buy is that big obstacle most homeowners face: securing a large down payment. Additionally, there are closing costs involved, such as property tax, home inspections, insurance, application fees, and recording fees. Even if you bought a house that was selling below market value, you must also be prepared to spend money on some repairs or facelifts to make the house fit your living standards. You usually encounter and must pay for these costs even before you live a month in your home, not forgetting that you are also expected to pay your mortgage and insurance. These high upfront costs are some of the reasons some people hold off on home-ownership.

Less Mobility

Although this works both ways, as I positively mentioned above, owning your home grounds you in one place. Typically, homeowners are less likely to move around and explore different places to live. You may even be hesitant to look for work and other opportunities in different cities than the one in which you reside. It is time-consuming and not always feasible to sell a house when you have to relocate for an opportunity in another state or city. This might also involve giving up great education options for your kids, and it can be expensive to have members of the family periodically travel out of town. Moreover, homeowners are also less likely to take vacations as a larger portion of their budget goes toward keeping their home.

Maintenance Costs

Being a homeowner means owning the property and all its potential problems. You must budget time and money for landscaping, plumbing, electrical, and structural maintenance. If anything breaks, leaks, or gets damaged in any way, it is your responsibility to fix it to avoid any further problems.

Equity Does Not Grow Immediately

It is worth noting that your equity does not grow immediately because a significant portion of your monthly payments go toward the interest on the loan. It could take a few years before you have a substantial percentage of ownership; therefore, the benefits of having equity will only be visible later.

Opportunity Cost

Opportunity cost essentially means the potential benefits that you forfeit by investing in a specific asset versus the alternative. With homeownership, the money that you could be using for other investments with a possibly quicker return is now invested in your down payment and closing costs. You may have to let those other opportunities pass you by as your money it tied up in your house. If homeownership is a better deal for you, then what you let pass you by will not matter.

Continuing Costs

While the mortgage rate is usually fixed, giving you predictable costs to help you properly budget your finances, there are additional expenses to account for. Property tax, homeowners insurance, utilities, and maintenance are ongoing costs. Are you prepared for more than just your mortgage payment? It is also worth noting that not all mortgages have a fixed rate; others have adjustable rates and periods. Therefore, it is wise to budget for these varying and unexpected expenses.

Market Risk

As with any investment, the housing economy is also characterized by the market's swings. Therefore, you will need to be prepared when the property market is in a downturn, as it means the value of your home will be declining. A worst-case scenario is having negative equity—also known as being underwater—when you end up owing more on your mortgage than the property is worth. This could be a big problem. If you had plans to sell the house in a downturn as you'd be forced to sell at a loss. If, however, you can ride it out and not try to sell or take equity out of your home during this time, you will be fine as over time the market will rise again and your equity will continue to build.

The Stress of Searching for a House

Limited Options

Knowing what you want in a home can be both a blessing and a curse. It should make it easier to avoid a home that doesn't meet your requirements. But, it can also be difficult if your options are limited. If you search in an area where few homes meet your criteria, it can cause a lot of stress.

Budget Constraints

Working with a tight budget can be a limiting factor as well. It can be stressful to forfeit a perfect home that exceeds your budget. On the other hand, compromising for another option because your first choice in house is too expensive can leave you with an unsatisfied feeling toward your home.

Uncertainty

The process of finding the right home is uncertain. There is no guarantee that you will find exactly what you are looking for, and that can cause anxiety. Even if you do get something you like, you cannot be certain that you will still feel the same about that house a few years down the line. You might also be wondering if it will meet your needs.

Emotional Turmoil

Searching for a house can be a thrilling process. Walking into open houses, falling in love with a potential home, and daydreaming about how your life will be in it can be exciting until you lose a bidding war or end up not qualifying for it. It is hard to rise from that disappointment and get over the emotional attachment you had to a particular house that you ended up not owning.

Time-Consuming

If you are searching for a house without the help of a professional agent, it can be like looking for a needle in a haystack. Going through multiple listing platforms, arranging for viewings, attending numerous open houses, and verifying deals can be time-consuming. Balancing this with other commitments can cause stress.

Psychology of Owning a Home

Generally, the feeling of owning a home has been associated with accomplishment and happiness. Feeling like you are living the American dream can bring joy and fulfillment. However, as with any material possession, research shows that this euphoria is short-lived and usually wears off once you get used to owning your home.

Why do it?

With all these negatives to homeownership, why do it? What's the point? The point is there is nothing like the feeling of owning your own home; nothing like the freedom to live as you want, to create your own sanctuary, to design it your way, to have your own dream life, to build a safe nest for your children, and to be secure in knowing you're sitting on an investment that will grow over time.

UNDERSTANDING THE BUYING PROCESS

Buying a home is one of the most important purchases you will have to make. Therefore, you must ensure that you fully understand the process to avoid making a purchase you regret. Below are some of the factors you have to consider for a smooth and less stressful activity.

Considering Your Financing Options

Before you even begin the search for the home that tickles your fancy and meets all your criteria, the first step is to evaluate your finances. How much do houses cost, and what is your budget? How much is required for a down payment? Ideally, 20% of the purchase price is expected. However, that depends on the type of financing you get. As a first-time buyer, there are several options that make it easier to qualify for financing if you have limited resources. For instance, you can qualify for several government-guaranteed loans—detailed in Chapter 5—and other state programs that require significantly lower to no down payments without attaching private mortgage insurance (PMI), as a traditional lender would typically require.

Preapprovals and Lender Choices

The next step is for you to get preapproved for a mortgage by contacting lenders. This means submitting essential documents, such as proof of income and employment, to potential lenders, who will then conduct a credit review to determine your financial standing and provide you with a preliminary loan estimate. A preapproval will give you a clear picture of your borrowing capacity and the potential interest rate you can expect to pay.

In addition to guiding you to shop for houses within the amount you can afford, it will also make your offer more appealing to sellers. When seeking preapproval or shopping around for a mortgage, it is crucial that you approach various financing authorities to evaluate the different options you have before settling on the first one at your disposal. Other things that will determine the type of financing you qualify for include your credit score, debt-to-income ratio, and proof of income, all of which are explained further in the book.

Finding a Home

Now that you're approved and know the amount a mortgage lender is willing to finance, the house search can begin. Again, congratulations on coming this far! Finding your ideal home can be an exciting process. Buckle up, though, as the road may be bumpy. A house search can entail a series of online searches through listing platforms, driving around your preferred neighborhood in search of "for sale" signs, or attending multiple open houses. You can also ask around and see if family, friends, and colleagues know of any houses for sale.

Or, you can take an easier approach and work with a professional real estate agent, as they can help match you with an available seller whose house meets your interests. Location preference, neighborhood, amenities, home size, type, and price range are some of the details you have to iron out before you start your search. Knowing what you want will narrow down your search so that you're not left confused with a wide range of properties that partly meet some of your interests. A good realtor will guide you through the maze of choices and help get you closer to your desired home.

Making an Offer

Once the house that best fits your needs is found, you are now ready to make an offer to purchase your home. However, do not be quick to throw money into a deal just yet. Work with a professional to make a comprehensive offer that meets all your requirements, with eyes wide open for opportunities to get a bargain. For instance, an agent might notice something with the deed that they can use to ask the seller to reduce the price. They have been in thousands of houses and handled many deals so they may see issues you would not notice. They may also know other seller concessions you can capitalize on to strike a better deal.

Inspecting a Home

With fresh paint and trimmed hedges, a house may look as good as new on the surface, yet there are underlying issues that are not instantly visible to a new and excited homebuyer. This is why you need a professional inspector to look for hidden flaws and possible areas where structural problems may hide until they later become apparent. Professionals can spot hidden termite damage or faulty wiring or plumbing issues, which may cost you later if you over-look them during inspection. While experts come at a price, they usually save you a lot of money on damages and repairs in the long run.

Closing the Deal

One of two things will happen: the inspection went smoothly and revealed that the house is flawless, or more likely, the inspection identified issues that need to be addressed. If there are undisclosed repairs or potential defects that may cost you in the future, you may then be able to negotiate a better deal. The seller may have to make those repairs or give you a discount for your future trouble. Alternatively, you can walk away from the deal if there are signifi-cant damages that the seller is refusing to work out in your favor.

All this is part of the negotiation and an experienced real estate agent is invaluable in this process. Once all items have been addressed to the satisfaction of both parties, you move toward the closing. Closing entails signing relevant paperwork that makes the purchase of transfer of ownership from the seller to you final and official. Closing costs often include appraisals, a title guarantee to ensure that no one else has a claim to the property, title insurance, an application fee, mortgage insurance and document recording fees.

After Closing

Congratulations! You're a homeowner. You can breathe a sigh of relief knowing that you have finally secured your dream home. However, the journey is not yet over. It is important that you keep your savings and expenses in check going forward. You now own the biggest possession, which comes with its own set of responsibilities. There are utilities, mortgages, insurance, renovations, and moving costs to pay. Of course, you should enjoy the peace that comes with homeownership and one of the ways you do this is to make sure you perform regular maintenance checks on your property. This will help you identify issues early before they require serious attention that could financially set you back.

THE IMPORTANCE OF HIRING EXPERTS

It is important to acknowledge that some people know best in areas where you may have little experience. The homebuying process requires you to engage professionals who will make it a less stressful journey for any beginner. Protect your investment and avoid mistakes by hiring and working with real estate experts for any process you are not confident navigating by yourself.

Avoid Costly Mistakes

It is crucial to not underestimate the importance of working with professional real estate agents. These experts have acquired enormous experience and know ways to avoid making costly mistakes. A deal may look good on paper, but only an expert can point out any hidden flaw you may have overlooked. You might have the upper hand to negotiate the purchase price based on the seller's concessions, but not recognize that opportunity and end up overpaying. An expert will help you look for opportunities to save money on a deal where you would otherwise be unaware of your bargaining chip.

Insight on Market Conditions

Considering market ups and downs, there are seasons that favor buyers over sellers and vice versa. If you are new to the property game, you may only look at current house prices and decide to purchase not knowing that prices could change in your benefit as the market changes. However, working with a professional agent can help steer you on the right path at the right time based on market conditions. Real estate agents also have access to market trends in a particular area that may vary from market trends in a different area; therefore, they can guide you on the best prices so that you lock in an optimal deal in a specific market condition.

Access to Unlisted Properties

At the time of your property search, not all homes for sale will be on the market. Your selection is limited to what is publicly available. However, real estate experts have access to undisclosed inventory, including houses that are yet to go on the market. If they know what you are looking for, they will help you find it, even if it means unearthing private deals that their colleagues are currently working on. As they have a network of other agents, they will contact other experts until they find the house you want and can advise you to wait for a particular house to go on the market before closing a deal with a property that does not meet your criteria.

Guidance on Purchase Price

Having shared your budget and your preapproved loan amount with an agent, you can rest assured that they will use the information to advise you on the purchase price. They will also factor in other details you mentioned, such as the location, accessibility, home size, number of bedrooms and bathrooms, and other relevant features, to ensure that you get your ideal home at the best possible price. They can even advise you on negotiation points to capitalize on and consider other bargains to sweeten the deal for you and the seller.

Error-Free Paperwork

Filling out relevant documents when buying a home requires meticulousness and insight. Legal documents like the sale agreement, title deed, and transfer details can be complicated and require an expert to interpret them in simpler terms. You want to ensure that you fill out the right documents correctly without any errors, which can be overwhelming if you do not have any experience or the right person in your corner guiding you.

Inexpensive for Buyers

Besides saving you a ton of money by avoiding costly mistakes, agents that facilitate the buying process are often inexpensive or even free for buyers. Both agents get most of their commission from sellers and developers. The job of a buyer's agent is to get you the house you want within your budget. The sale price of a house factors in the commission of both realtors, which is deducted from the seller's cut.

Action Steps:

How to Understand Homeownership Benefits:

❑ Learn about the advantages of owning a home, such as stability, investment potential, and tax benefits and list the benefits for you personally.

Assess Your Financial Readiness:

❑ Evaluate your financial situation, including mortgage options, to determine your readiness for homeownership. Thinking about the house you'd like to have, what would that house cost to buy and what type loan would you need to get to make that happen?

Recognize Potential Challenges:

❑ Be aware of potential obstacles like the house-hunting process and the complexities of buying a home. How can you prepare yourself to do what it takes to work through all the search and the purchase of your new home? What makes it worth it to you?

Seek Expert Guidance:

❑ Start searching for experts, like real estate agents and inspectors, to guide you, avoid costly mistakes, and navigate the market effectively. List the things you think experts could help you with in your search.

Now that you have officially started your homebuying journey by learning the benefits and challenges of the process, let's move on to the next chapter where you will find tools to assess your readiness to take action.

2

ASSESSING YOUR READINESS

With studies showing that 40% of Americans find the first-time homebuying process stressful and some regret their purchase (Gervis, 2018), what can you do to avoid this? One of the reasons behind this pressure is the fact that new homebuyers enter the market blindly, overlooking critical steps to assess their readiness for the demanding journey ahead. From searching for an ideal home to securing financing, going to multiple viewings, negotiating the price, and closing the deal, the process can seem endless.

In addition to confidence and decisiveness, it requires emotional, financial, and professional support to make it less overwhelming. So, it's wise to not underestimate the effort, time, and resources required to make homebuying blissful. This chapter will help you take a reality check and assess your position before you embark on this life-changing event.

ARE YOU READY TO BUY A HOUSE?

Contrary to the common belief that buying a house simply requires being ready financially and finding the right location, there are several things to consider before finalizing that purchase, even if you can afford it. The season you are buying in, the local housing market trends, your lifestyle needs, debt, income stability, and the economy in general play a vital role in determining your readiness. If you are buying with a mortgage, these factors also affect the amount for which you will qualify and what lenders expect the percentage of your income to be for house-related expenses only.

Understand Your Debt-To-Income Ratio

It's pretty simple: the debt-to-income (DTI) ratio means the amount of debt you are paying versus the money you are earning. It is an essential measure that lenders use to evaluate your financial standing and your capability to pay debt every month. Your DTI ratio will determine your mortgage approval; therefore, it is one of the measures you must be concerned about when assessing your readiness to buy a house. You can reduce this ratio by increasing your income, which is usually the hardest part, or by decreasing your overall debt. Even if you have low debt, this is still a determining factor in the amount of mortgage for which you qualify. Your DTI ratio also indirectly affects the location and size of the house you will buy, as those are both determined by price.

Can You Afford the Down Payment?

Naturally, your deposit amount will affect your readiness to buy a house. Your down payment determines the monthly mortgage payments and interest rate of the loan. Depending on the type of lender, you will typically pay more for a mortgage if you have less or no down payment. The opposite is true; if you have a substantial down payment, your monthly mortgage will significantly reduce, and lenders will offer you a lower interest rate. Having a sizable down payment indicates that you have some skin in the game and lenders will find you to be a safe bet compared to someone who puts in little to no down payment.

Some of the benefits of a large down payment include building equity, which works in your favor when tapping into equity loans or lines of credit if you have other financial needs. Putting down a large deposit will reduce or waive the PMI in conventional loans or the mortgage insurance premiums (MIPs) in the case of Federal Housing Administration (FHA)-approved loans.

Remember, you can also apply for a government-guaranteed loan that offers 100% financing if you meet the requirements.

Do You Have a Reliable Source of Income?

It is important to remember that having a place to live is one of the longest commitments you will face and this requires a stable source of income. While renting comes with the flexibility that you can change places whenever your financial situation changes, homeownership does not. Of course, you can downsize your home when the going gets tough.

To pay for your perfect home, your mortgage will usually be around 30 years long. This requires you to have a stable job or a solid income stream that can weather any economic tsunami. Before you start your homeownership quest, you must think ahead and consider how you will make future mortgage payments.

Consider Your Lifestyle Needs

Your lifestyle needs to play a vital role in determining your readiness to own a home. You must factor in several life events that can affect the size of the home you need. For instance, if you are planning to expand your family, either through more children or taking in relatives to live with you long-term, you will need a bigger house than if you have a smaller family. Similarly, if you already have children, you may want to consider a house in a neighborhood that has better schools.

Your children's future education might also influence your home-buying decision. If they are going to college soon, you might want to have money on standby for those needs and choose a less expensive house. You may also want to put off house shopping if you have other pressing responsibilities to pay. Considering your current and future plans will help you to not bite off more than you can chew or take on financially demanding responsibilities without leaving room to breathe.

Consider Your Future Plans

How do your future plans impact your readiness to buy a home? The length of time you intend to own the house, impending financial obligations, and possible career and life changes can influence your decision. While looking at your immediate needs is often a deciding factor, you must also consider your future plans because they help you determine the type and size of property you choose. Your future plans may also determine your down payment if you know the house you're buying is only temporary and your future plans are to move to another city where you will plant long-term roots. Moreover, if you plan to use your house as an investment, you may also want to take this into consideration, as it will play a role in how you use your equity to refinance the mortgage or to plan your general exit strategy.

Does the Housing Market Favor Renting Over Buying?

We have already established that owning a home is a long-term financial commitment that does not end with a down payment, closing costs, or mortgage but also includes maintaining the house in the long run. Therefore, even if you had plans to settle in your own home, if the housing market is more favorable to renting, it may be wise to wait to buy. However, if rental prices are on the rise, buying might be a better option, whereas if home prices are rising, renting might be ideal. The latest National Association of Realtors (NAR) report reflects that the current housing market may be more favorable for buyers as sales hit the lowest in 13 years due to increased home prices (Mutikani, 2023).

While high prices indicate that entry into the housing market is difficult for first-time homeowners, the projections reflect that prices are likely to continue rising, making homebuying now a good investment. However, if you think putting off buying for now will work more in your favor, you can wait and opt for renting until you are ready. It is important to be realistic and not put yourself under unnecessary pressure to buy now only to regret it later. Therefore, the decision to buy or rent is entirely up to you as you weigh the pros and cons of each, which I share toward the end of this chapter.

The Economic Overview

So, how will economics affect your decision? Is it the right time to buy?

Similar to the housing market effect, the general economic overview can reflect whether or not buying a house is ideal. First, the current economy as I write, may be difficult for first-time homebuyers due to the inflated house prices. Is the next season a better time to buy? It could be, if the number of sales drop and inventories increase, as this might force sellers to also drop their selling price.

The seller's market, on the other hand, means that houses have increased in value and are more profitable to sell than to buy. So, before you make an offer to purchase, consider the season and the economy. Work with a professional. No one has a crystal ball, but seasoned real estate agents have been around long enough to recognize the trends and are ready to help you realize your goals at the time that makes the most sense for you.

And then there's the money piece: interest rates and the time of year are factors that can determine the economic outlook.

Let's look at how these factors affected David, a first time home-buyer. He sat down with his friend Jack, a real estate agent, to talk about markets and when it's best to buy.

"If interest rates go up," Jack said, "fewer people get loans, and then houses aren't selling, so there are fewer houses on the market. That can be good for you as a buyer, because property prices can drop. In that type of market it makes sense to make a purchase sooner rather than later to take advantage of the lower house prices. Just be aware there may be fewer houses to choose from."

David, who works in the financial markets, feels sure that rates will stay low. "If that happens," says Jack, "then you have two options. One is to put off buying for a while because falling interest rates means more people will get loans, and there could be bidding wars on the houses on the market which will likely mean house prices will go up."

"But," says David, "isn't it better to get a loan when rates are low?"

"Yes, generally, it is," says David, "because falling interest rates also make loan payments smaller, so your second option is to buy now as those lower rates mean you might get into a larger house even though the house prices are high."

The next logical step was for Jack to connect David with a reputable lender to help him work through his finances to deter-mine how much house payment David could afford and how the current market would affect his loan rate.

All together, David was smart, and so would you be, to analyze how the seasons of the year affect inventories and home prices in your area. The hot buying season may include people having money to make big purchases so that they can celebrate important milestones in their own homes, which would drive prices up. Cooler selling seasons may come with low sales and potentially falling prices which is good for buyers, but it may mean fewer houses on the market.

ARE YOU EMOTIONALLY READY?

Buying a home is not just a business transaction because it entails so much more. This is where you will build a life full of memorable experiences. It is typical that you may form an emotional connection with a house. This can influence your decision, and you may end up overpaying for a home or not negotiating rationally because your emotions are on high alert. While your instincts might occasionally be correct, there are times when making an emotional decision can cost you financially if you overlook other factors. Therefore, it is important to regulate your emotions so that they do not overrule your decisions.

Do Not Take Rejection Personally

Once you have found the right house and you can see your family happily living there, that's not a guarantee that things will go as planned. It's possible your offer for that dream home is not accepted. Perhaps the seller found a better offer than yours, so yours got rejected. The sense of loss can lead to a lot of unhappiness and dissatisfaction with the house you end up getting.

It is important to understand that this is a business transaction; it's a win-or-lose game. There's no advantage to taking the loss personally where you sulk over the house you did not get. Sure, you're allowed to feel sad and even mourn a loss, but move on. Keep your head in the game and focus on what is next coming your way. The next offer on another house might even be better when you consider all the other aspects.

Do Not Be Afraid to Walk Away

Just as it is important to not take rejection to heart, you must be able to know when to move on from a deal. Whether it falls through because the seller went with another offer or your financing came short, you must know when to accept defeat and look for another win elsewhere. Seeing that other offers are higher, you may be tempted to overspend just to win the deal. Warning! This is a costly move that can negatively affect the rest of your financial planning for years to come.

Don't be tempted to make an impulsive decision by letting your emotions get in the way. If you disregard your budget because of emotions, you may still end up with buyer's remorse anyway. So, don't be afraid to walk away and start the search all over again until you find what meets both your needs and your budget. You'll be happier in the long run.

Trust Your Realtor

One of the best ways to avoid making emotional decisions is by working with a professional realtor. It's one of the best kept secrets: your real estate agent becomes that buffer between you and rash decisions. You can rest assured that they know the insights of the market and can tell whether or not a deal is good. Professionals are able to focus on deals that make financial sense instead of dwelling on emotions. They can also help you focus on your needs versus your wants when choosing your home. Realtors have experience in negotiating better deals. They also thoroughly know the neighborhood and can advise you on what to be prepared for to avoid surprises.

It is important to trust your realtor and lean on them for support because it is their job to have your best interests at heart. They will consider them during the search for your home and in negotiations for a better price. Therefore, it's best to start a journey with a professional realtor to ensure that you do not make any costly emotional decisions you may regret later.

USING A MORTGAGE CALCULATOR

As a first-time homebuyer, sometimes it can be hard to know what to expect when buying a home. Particularly, knowing the price range for your ideal home, possible loan types and their differences, and estimating the required down payment may be overwhelming. Fortunately, there are resourceful tools, such as a mortgage calculator, that can help you predict the financial requirements of your home and properly plan your budget.

What Is a Mortgage Calculator?

A mortgage calculator is a financial tool that helps borrowers estimate their potential monthly mortgage payments and other key details associated with a mortgage loan. It is a valuable resource you can use when buying a home, as it provides insights into the financial aspects of homeownership. It also helps you determine how much you can expect to pay for the duration of your loan, making budgeting easier.

What Can It Do?

Determine Price Range

A mortgage calculator can help you estimate the financial requirements involved in homeownership. You can use it to evaluate how adjusting the loan amount, down payment, interest rate, loan period, and other housing-related expenses will affect your monthly payments.

Compare Loan Types and Terms

You can use a mortgage calculator to evaluate different loan types, such as fixed- and adjustable-rate mortgages (FRM and ARM), to see how much each will cost you over its term. An FRM will likely indicate a predictable amount you will pay over the course of the loan, while an ARM will be variable.

Generate Amortization Schedules

A mortgage calculator can also generate amortization schedules, which allow you to see a detailed breakdown of each mortgage payment over time. You can see how much goes toward principal and interest, homeowners insurance, PMI, property tax, and homeowners association (HOA) fees, where applicable.

Start Budgeting

A mortgage calculator allows you to adjust different amounts so that you can see what makes the most impact and where you need to channel your money and stay within your budget.

Knowing how all the different figures for your mortgage and house-related expenses affect your monthly payment will help you budget your money wisely in the long run.

Indicate the Impact of Your Down Payment

You can see how changing the down payment amount affects the monthly payment. If you do not put down any deposit on your house, the monthly payment will be steeper than when you increase your down payment. The higher the percentage or amount of your down payment, the lower your monthly payment will be.

How to Use a Mortgage Calculator

To use a mortgage calculator, you will need to input relevant information such as loan amount, down payment, interest, property tax, homeowners insurance, loan term, and other variables. Adjusting any of the figures or scenarios affects the monthly payment, giving you a rough estimate of how much you are expected to pay for your home. You can then review the results of experimenting with different scenarios until you find the one that meets your affordability. You can also use a mortgage calculator in the following 12 steps:

1. **Loan type:** Start by selecting the type of loan you are applying for. For instance, as a first-time applicant, you will choose a home purchase loan over other types of loans, such as refinancing an existing mortgage or cash-out refinance.

2. **Property value:** The second thing you will input into the calculator is the price of the home you are applying for. You can obtain this information from the property listing or the most recent appraisal.

3. **Down payment:** Being one of the most important factors that will affect your monthly payment and interest, the next value you will enter on the calculator is the amount of down payment you plan to make. In the case of mortgage refinancing, you will insert the mortgage balance.

4. **Property ZIP Code:** Enter the correct ZIP Code of your county for the mortgage calculator to get the right property tax rates.

5. **Credit score:** You must also provide your current credit score, which will determine the loan product and interest rate for which you qualify. Ideally, a credit score of 740 or above will qualify for the lowest interest rates.

6. **Home loan goals:** You will adjust the mortgage calculator depending on your home loan goals. If your target is to pay a low interest rate regardless of the loan term, you will input the rate you want, and the calculator will factor it into the monthly payment. You can also desire to pay the lowest monthly payment, which will likely require a sizable down payment and a longer loan term. Other goals

may include paying an FRM or ARM for a predictable budget or short-term ownership, respectively.

7. **Property type:** If you want property type-specific financing, you must select the advanced option on a mortgage calculator to answer relevant questions related to the property type of your choice. From single-family, two-family, three-family, and four-family homes to condominiums and housing cooperatives (co-ops), different lenders offer variable interest rates. Therefore, you must select the exact property type you plan to finance.

8. **Property purpose:** Indicate how you plan to use the property to determine the loan interest rates you will qualify for. Lenders typically charge higher interest on investment properties than those intended for primary residence.

9. **Personal information:** Indicate if you are a U.S. citizen or a first-time homebuyer in order to qualify for specific loan products that may offer low down payment and closing-cost options. You could qualify for an FHA loan if you meet both criteria.

10. **Property taxes:** It is common for lenders to charge one-twelfth of your annual tax, include it in your monthly payment, and then pay it to your county when the bill comes due. Find out if your lender pays property tax on your behalf or if you must do it directly with your county.

11. **Homeowners insurance:** To protect your house from any disasters, you must pay homeowners insurance. This is also a prerequisite for lenders to protect their investment in you. You can contact your insurance provider for the correct premium amount, which is often based on the value of your home. Lenders also usually charge this in

your monthly payment and pay the insurance on your behalf when the bill comes due.

12. **HOA fees:** You will need to pay HOA fees if your home is part of a shared property, like a condominium or townhouse, where you share some amenities with other homeowners. Leave this section blank if your home is on a separate property and there are no HOA fees.

13. **Calculate your monthly mortgage payment:** Finally, review that you input the correct information, and then press the button to get your mortgage options. If you are happy with any of the provided options, you can go ahead and start an online application process for mortgage prequalification.

We live in the technological age, baby, and all these tools are readily available online. Have fun going through the different loan options!

TO RENT OR TO BUY?

The key difference between buying and renting lies in the ownership of the property. As a homeowner, you have full ownership rights and control over the property, whereas being a tenant only grants you temporary rights to property usage. Buying comes with freedom and responsibility, while renting involves restrictions and less responsibility for the property.

As I mentioned earlier, there will be times you are faced with a choice between renting or buying a home, especially due to market conditions. While your goal is to have a place called "home," the conditions may be unfavorable at that time, requiring you to stick to renting. Perhaps the following benefits and drawbacks of renting versus the ones addressed for buying in the previous chapter can help determine your readiness and influence your decision.

Benefits of Renting

Less Upfront Costs

Although most landlords require the first and last months' rent and the security deposit, this amount is a drop in the ocean compared to the down payment and closing costs required for homeownership.

Mobility

Renting comes with the flexibility to move to and explore other cities and careers without any worries other than whether to break your lease or plan to move as your lease expires. Moving out of a rented property is easier than having to sell your home to relocate to another area.

Maintenance and Repairs Are Not Your Responsibility

While you may still be asked to handle minor damages to a property, major maintenance and repairs are the responsibility of a homeowner and not yours as a tenant.

No Property Tax Bills

Like maintenance, property taxes are not your responsibility but that of the landlord.

No Need to Worry About Declining Home Values

When home prices are falling and owners are worried about losing their investment, you have no worries as a tenant because none of it affects you.

Paying Rent May Help Build Your Credit

Although not all landlords report rent to the credit bureaus, those that are reported can help build your credit profile.

Drawbacks of Renting

Increasing Rent

Unlike fixed-rate mortgages, rent may increase at the sole discretion of the landlord, and there is nothing you can do about it.

Restrictions Over the Property

You are granted limited rights to the property, meaning you cannot do as you please as you would if you were the owner. You cannot remodel or design the property according to your taste.

Risk of Displacement If the Landlord Decides to Sell the Property

Should the seller receive a tempting offer to sell the property, you may have very short notice to find a new place to stay, which can be inconvenient.

You Get Nothing at the End of Your Lease

Instead of building equity with your monthly payment, your rent is helping the landlord pay off the mortgage he owes. In the end, the landlord ends up owning the property free and clear, while you get to the end of your rental agreement with nothing. The homeowner is making money out of your rent because their home is an investment, but to you, it is just an expense that you usually have no right to even sublease.

No Tax Benefits

Unlike a homeowner who has tax benefits, you cannot use the amount you paid in rent to reduce your tax liability. Both renting and buying have varying benefits and drawbacks. Eventually, it all comes down to your goals and financial situation. It is up to you to decide which one fits you best. If you are ready to handle the financial, emotional, and physical responsibilities and commitments of homeownership, buying may be ideal. Whereas, if you still want to maintain your freedom and hold on to your savings for other things other than being tied down to a home investment, renting might be a good option.

BIGGER HOUSE OR SMALLER MORTGAGE?

Sometimes, you may be in a dilemma between home size and loan amount. A bigger house means a bigger mortgage, and the same logic is true for a smaller house. You have to choose your options correctly to fit into your financial landscape and monthly budget. The following reasons will help you decide on your home size.

Reasons to Buy a Bigger Home

Growing Family

If you are planning on a bigger family, getting a bigger house makes sense so that your growing family can have more room to live.

Leasing Part of Your House

Perhaps you saw a business opportunity and decided to use part of your house as a rental. You can either have long-term tenants or nightly guests by listing your rental space on popular sites like Airbnb.

Home Office Option

If you are working from home, like many people have since the pandemic-imposed lockdowns, getting a bigger house allows you to turn an extra bedroom or any free space into an office.

More Outdoor Space

A house with a big yard can also allow you to host family and friend gatherings as well as allow your children the freedom to play outdoors.

Reasons to Go for a Smaller Home

Affordable Location

Bigger houses are usually located in upscale areas where affordability might be an issue. Your commute, kids' schools, and other amenities in a suburban area also do not come cheap. Therefore, getting a house in your preferred upmarket location might be a financial burden. A smaller house, on the other hand, is likely to be in an affordable neighborhood.

Low Upfront and Continuing Costs

A smaller house comes with a smaller mortgage, a lower down payment, property tax, homeowner's insurance, and possibly lower utility bills. Compared to a big house, maintaining a smaller house is also way more affordable. Therefore, if you want a house that fits your current and future budget, a smaller house might be your best bet.

Fewer Responsibilities

Keeping a smaller house means less outdoor space and lower maintenance than that of a bigger house. A bigger house requires more effort to maintain in good condition and, therefore, takes more responsibility.

A Bigger Home Is Not a Guaranteed Investment

A smaller house is a great investment that attracts most investors because it has a better resale value and offers better chances to remodel. Contrarily, a bigger house already has a limited number of buyers—those who can afford it. A bigger house is not a guaranteed investment, as its high price may limit its resale value.

Your readiness to buy a home is determined by your financial resources: your income, down payment, and debt management. You must also assess your emotional readiness for taking this big step. Weighing the pros and cons of renting versus buying can also help you decide if you are ready.

Action Steps

Financial Readiness

❏ Evaluate Your Finances - List the items you need to collect to understand your financial situation, including income, savings, and debts.

Affordability and Future Plans

❏ Determine Affordability - When you pull all your records together, what does the picture of your finances and your stable income tell you? What, if anything, needs to change?
❏ Consider Lifestyle and Goals - Think about your lifestyle needs and long-term plans. How do your finances fit into those goals?

Market and Emotions

❏ Analyze the Housing Market - Research the current
market conditions in the area in which you'd like to live.
❏ Emotional Readiness - What do your emotional reactions
to the market and to the process tell you about your readiness to handle homeownership? What will it take to set
emotion aside and think logically through the process?

Decision-Making Tools

❏ Use Mortgage Calculators - Learn how to use mortgage
calculators to estimate costs. Do the Rent vs. Buy
Comparison - Compare the pros and cons of renting and
buying, considering your preferences and financial
situation.

Read on! The following chapter will focus on helping you budget
your finances for your best success.

3

BUDGETING

With 57% of homeowners worried about future repair costs of their homes and 23% without any emergency funds for unexpected costs, it is apparent that most homebuyers start their journey blindly (Roughley, 2022). Unexpected costs can skyrocket and leave any unprepared owner in financial ruin. To avoid this, it is paramount to join this club of homebuyer's with your eyes open and ready to tackle the financial responsibilities that come with homeownership. One of the key strategies is to stick to a budget and review it from time to time to ensure that you allocate enough finances to comfortably keep and maintain your home without stress. So, let's dive in as this chapter succinctly addresses budgeting and financial preparedness for the continuing costs of homeownership.

RESPONSIBILITIES OF HOMEOWNERSHIP

Before you bite off more than you can chew by underestimating the continuing costs of your new property, it is crucial to take on the following responsibilities that come with homeownership. From expected monthly payments to regular maintenance costs, the goal is to be financially prepared to spend money on your home. Knowing your responsibilities and potential costs will help you avoid a financial setback that catches you by surprise.

Mortgage Payments

While a tenant may get away with an excuse for not paying rent one month or making a late payment, you don't have that luxury as a homeowner. One of your primary responsibilities is to consistently pay your mortgage on time. As one of my attorney friends who handled many of my closings was fond of saying, "If you don't pay, you can't stay!"

Housing-Related Costs

From property taxes to PMI and homeowners insurance, you are liable to pay all applicable housing-related costs.

Regular Home Repairs and Maintenance Costs

Renters live worry-free, knowing that any repairs or maintenance are not their responsibility. That's the upside of renting and most of us know people affected by the downside, which is that some landlords make no repairs or improvements and their tenants find themselves living in decaying properties.

As a homeowner, however, if you act like a bad landlord and do no maintenance or repairs, you can't just walk away from a decaying house like you can an apartment. Deferred maintenance can swallow you whole as the minor repair issues become major disasters. The sooner you schedule regular home repairs and maintenance, the sooner you will avoid any further damage to your property.

The following cost estimates for repairs will help you allocate enough funds to cover scheduled maintenance and emergency repair costs.

Most Common Repair Costs

Foundation

The foundation is the most important part of your house and can be costly when damaged. The condition of your foundation is one of the main reasons you need a home inspections to alert you to any hidden issues that might worsen later. Any issues around it must be immediately taken care of to avoid further structural damage to your home. Making foundation repairs can cost around $10,000 or more (Luna, 2022).

Electrical

Electrical issues are best left to professionals to avoid any costly accidents; it wouldn't be wise to compromise by trying to handle them yourself. You can expect to pay around $100–$400 on minor repairs and $2,500 to replace an electrical panel for major issues.

Roofing

Like the foundation, the roof of your house also requires special attention and immediate action whenever there are issues. The sooner you address a leaking roof, the more money you will save by avoiding an entire roof replacement. Taking regular, low-cost preventative measures, like gutter cleaning, will save you major damage. Minor roof repairs would likely cost about $950, while full roof replacements would cost up to $8,000.

Water Heater

Water heaters are some of those items you can expect to repair regularly or replace at some point due to mineral buildup and periodic breakdowns. You can budget $600 to fix a water heater or $1,700 to replace it.

Water Damage

Similar to electrical issues, it is wise to contact a professional plumber to handle any water damage because of their better understanding of pipelines and how water flows around the property. Whether it is a burst or leaky pipe or damage from a storm, water damage usually affects the wall, ceiling, flooring, and more areas. A professional will know how and where to fix it to avoid repeating the problem. While the costs of repair depend on the size of the affected area, you can budget around $2,600 to fix the damage.

Septic System Repair

Not only is restoring the proper functionality of the sewage system a dirty job, but it also comes at premium prices. Replacing a new sewer line may cost around $5,000–6,000, while fixing any related plumbing issues ranges from $600–1,750.

Heating Ventilation and Air Conditioning Repairs

Whether you are living in a region that experiences extreme weather or not, having a fully functional heating, ventilation and air conditioning (HVAC) system is one of the best home investments. While a new energy-efficient unit must ideally last 12–15 years, replacing it is often more worthwhile than regularly fixing the old one. You can expect to pay $350 to fix an AC unit or $4,500 to install the furnace.

Termite Control

It is important to get a pest control expert to help you get rid of termites as soon as you realize they're there because they eat away at your structure. Treating termites can cost around $575, while an infestation can cause $3,000 worth of damage. A termite-damaged house can affect the resale value of your property; therefore, you must deal with termites as soon as possible.

Mold Removal

Mold, usually occurring as a result of water damage or moisture, must be immediately dealt with because of its potential health problems, especially in small children. While minor mold problems can be removed with mold removal products, bleach, or soapy water, it is important to call in a professional if a problem persists. You can budget about $2,500 for mold removal in adverse situations.

The Average Costs of Home Repairs

Since estimating future costs of damages is only an estimate, some experts recommend following the following rules of thumb.

The 1% Rule

It is considered wise to set aside at least 1% of your home's value for maintenance or house-related emergency costs. For instance, if your home is worth $450,000, you will need to budget $4,500 or more per year for repairs and maintenance.

The 10% Rule

It is also recommended that you budget an extra 10% of your monthly housing-related costs, including your mortgage, property tax, and homeowners insurance. If you spend $1,200 on your mortgage, $200 on tax, and $100 on insurance, then you must have a minimum of $150 per month.

The Square-Foot Rule

To get a near-accurate estimate of the money you should budget for maintenance and repairs, you can use the size of your home because size also matters. Put aside $1 per square foot of your livable space. For instance, John and Paula must save aside $3,000 a year for their 3,000-sq-ft home, while Dave and Maria would need to budget $208 per month or $2,500 to repair a 2,500-sq-ft home.

THE HOUSING EXPENSE RATIO

The housing expense ratio, also known as the front-end ratio, is a crucial financial metric that lenders use to evaluate a borrower's capacity to handle housing-related costs, especially their mortgage payment. Although the housing expense ratio is part of the DTI ratio, which lenders consider when evaluating mortgage applications, it is important to distinguish between the two. The DTI ratio covers the overall borrower's debt obligations against pretax income, while the housing expense ratio only focuses on housing-related costs.

As a rule of thumb, FHA mortgages typically require the borrower to keep the DTI ratio at 43% or below. This means that your general debt, inclusive of housing-related expenses, should not be more than 43% of your gross monthly income. However, most lenders with stricter criteria require that your front-end DTI ratio, which is limited to housing-related costs, be kept at no more than 28% of your income (Gobel, 2022).

How to Calculate Your Housing Expense Ratio

The housing expense ratio is calculated by adding all monthly housing costs and dividing by gross monthly income before taxes and other deductions. The goal is to have this ratio, which is often expressed as a percentage, in a range that lenders consider manageable. Typically, if you keep this ratio around 28% or below, lenders will see that you are responsible and that you can manage debt well.

Understanding and calculating your housing expense ratio is a useful exercise when preparing to apply for a mortgage. It helps you assess whether your housing costs align with your income and what lenders typically consider acceptable. It is worth noting that while the housing expense ratio is an essential factor in mortgage qualification, lenders also evaluate your overall DTI ratio, which includes all your monthly debt obligations, not just housing-related expenses.

Example:

Let's say Tom earns $5,000 per month. His current mortgage is $1,500 for the principal and interest, and he pays homeowners insurance of $100, property taxes of $300, and his utilities are $200 per month. Adding all these housing-related costs, Tom's monthly expenses are $2,100.

On the other hand, Emily earns $6,000 per month. She pays a mortgage of $1,200, $200 in tax, $120 in utilities, and $80 in insurance. Her total monthly housing expenses equal $1,600.

Housing expense ratio = (Total housing costs) / (Monthly gross income) x 100

In Tom's case: $2,100/$5,000 x 100 = 42%

In Emily's scenario: $1,600/$6,000 x 100 = 26.7%

When both Tom and Emily are applying for financing, most lenders will reject Tom's application due to his high housing expense ratio, while Emily stands a better chance of approval because her ratio falls within the acceptable threshold. Even if Tom were to apply for an FHA loan, that would mean the rest of his debt obligations would need to be at most 1% to make a total of 43%, which is highly impossible.

BUILDING A REALISTIC BUDGET

Budgeting essentially helps you understand how money flows to and from you. As you embark on your homebuying journey, it is crucial to plan how you spend the money you earn to afford your living costs and make future financial preparations.

Benefits of Budgeting

Determining Affordability

A budget helps you figure out how much you can afford to spend on a home. It considers your income, existing debts, and other expenses. It prevents you from going into financial ruin or spending more money than you can afford.

Setting Realistic Goals

A budget allows you to set realistic homebuying goals. It helps you decide whether you are looking for a starter home, a larger family home, or an investment property, and how long it will take to save for a down payment.

Savings and Down Payment

Budgeting helps you save for a down payment. As I said earlier, a larger down payment often leads to better mortgage terms, such as lower interest rates and reduced monthly payments.

Estimating Total Costs

Beyond the purchase price, there are various costs associated with buying a home, such as closing costs, property taxes, insurance, and ongoing maintenance. A budget ensures you consider all these expenses.

Choosing the Right Mortgage

Your budget will help you select the right mortgage type and terms. It influences whether you opt for an FRM or ARM and for how long.

Avoiding Overcommitment

Without a budget, it is easy to become enamored with a property that is beyond your financial means. A budget helps you stay within your comfort zone and avoid being house-poor, where too much of your income goes toward housing costs.

Long-Term Financial Health

Your budget should account for ongoing homeownership costs, such as property taxes, insurance, utilities, and maintenance. This ensures you are prepared for the long-term financial commitment of homeownership.

Negotiating Power

When you know what you can afford and have a budget in place, you are in a stronger position when negotiating with sellers and lenders.

Financial Flexibility and Preparedness

A budget allows you to adapt to unexpected changes in your financial situation, such as job loss or increased expenses.

Investment Goals

Your budget should align with your long-term financial goals. If buying a home is part of your investment strategy, your budget will help ensure that your investment supports your overall financial plan.

Getting Organized

Gather Financial Information

Collect all your financial documents, including bank statements, pay stubs, bills, credit card statements, and any other relevant financial records. You need a complete picture of your income, expenses, and debts.

Identify All Your Income Sources

List all sources of income, including your salary, freelance work, rental income, investment dividends, and any other money that comes in regularly. How much money flows to you generally?

List Expenses

Categorize your expenses into fixed, variable, and discretionary categories. Fixed expenses are those that are unlikely to change and include rent or mortgage, utilities, and insurance. Variable expenses may fluctuate month-to-month and include groceries and medical bills. Discretionary expenses are those nice-to-haves, such as entertainment, going to movies, and dining out.

Determine Specific Amounts

For each expense category, determine how much you typically spend each month. You can use past bank and credit card statements as references.

Set Budget Limits

Establish spending limits for each category based on your financial goals. Ideally, your total expenses must not exceed your income. You must leave a breathing space between what you earn and what you spend your money on. For instance, if your income is $4,500 a month, you want to keep your entire expenses around $3,500 or below and not maximize all your earnings. By expenses, I mean all your financial obligations here, not just your housing costs or debt.

Emergency Fund and Savings

Include categories for saving, such as an emergency fund, retirement accounts, and other savings goals. Allocate funds to an emergency fund and work toward long-term financial goals, like paying down debt or saving for a big purchase. Saving money should be a nonnegotiable part of your budget.

Tracking Tools

Choose a tracking tool that works for you. This can be a spreadsheet, budgeting software like Mint or You Need A Budget (YNAB), or even a simple pen-and-paper system. The tool should help you record income and expenses. You can also automate your budget where possible. Set up automatic transfers to savings accounts or investments to avoid any temptation or default. This ensures that you are consistently saving and investing without relying solely on willpower.

Regularly Update

Commit to regularly updating your budget. You can choose a frequency that suits your needs, whether it's daily, weekly, or monthly. You must also monitor and adjust your budget as you see fit. Review to see how your actual spending compares to your budgeted amounts. If you are overspending in one category, adjust your spending in another to compensate. Your budget is a flexible tool that you can adjust from time to time.

How to Set a Budget

Consider the 28% Rule

If you do not know where to start when setting up a budget for your home, the 28% rule can be your guide. Knowing that you must limit your housing-related expenses to 28% is a good foundation. Besides being a prerequisite for mortgage qualification for most lenders, the 28% rule helps you stay on top of your finances. If your homeownership costs are kept at this ratio, they leave more room for other financial obligations in your budget.

Do Not Limit Your Budget Only to Mortgage Payments

As I mentioned earlier, there are several other housing-related expenses beyond your mortgage payments. Property taxes, homeowners insurance, HOA fees, utilities, repairs, and any maintenance costs must all be part of your housing budget. Keeping your lawns manicured, your yard tidy, and your gutters free from any leaves comes at a cost. During snow season, you have to shovel snow out of the way, and that may also costs money. It is crucial to consider the total amount of money allocated to these homeownership costs. Being realistic about your total monthly homeownership costs will help you manage your finances better and make adjustments where necessary.

Let Your Down Payment Determine Your Purchase Price

If you cannot put down a large deposit, you must be prepared for the fact that your monthly mortgage payments will be greater. Considering the huge interest rate and possibly PMI or MIP, your monthly obligations will be more than for someone who paid a sizable down payment. Maybe this is an indication that you must go for a lower mortgage that will fit your budget. If you have been able to save enough for a down payment, then you can go for the house whose mortgage and continuing costs fit your budget.

Choose a Property You Can Handle

While having a bigger house in a great location sounds like a dream, it is crucial that you choose a property you can handle. Always look ahead and consider the work that comes with owning a particular property in terms of its size and condition. Maintaining a large home can be problematic in extreme weather, as heating or cooling can be quite costly. The bigger the size, the bigger the responsibility. Additionally, if you are not up for extensive renovations, stay away from a fixer-upper, even if it comes at a lower cost. You want a house you can afford effortlessly, which fits your budget and time investment.

USING A BUDGET TEMPLATE

Using a budget template is a practical and efficient way to manage your finances. It ensures that budgeting and keeping track of your finances are not complicated tasks, even for beginners. The good news is that there are numerous free-to-use budget templates available online that you can either download or directly use from the website. Below is a detailed guide on how to use a budget template.

Step 1: Choose or Create a Budget Template

You can find numerous budget templates online. Popular choices include spreadsheets like Microsoft Excel or Google Sheets, budgeting apps, or even pen-and-paper templates. Choose one that suits your preferences and needs. If you prefer, you can create a custom budget template tailored to your specific financial situation. You can do this by using spreadsheet software like the mentioned Excel or Google Sheets. While this can be fun, it can also be tedious if you have to manually update it every month.

Step 2: Gather Financial Information

Begin by documenting all your sources of income. Include your salary, freelance work, rental income, investment dividends, and any other regular income streams. Be sure to note the amounts and frequencies. Next, you must organize your expenses into fixed and variable categories. You must have a tab or section that clearly articulates your unchanging costs, such as rent or mortgage, utilities, insurance, and loan payments.

You must also do the same with your more flexible costs, like groceries, dining out, entertainment, and discretionary spending. You can either list all your variable expenses or create categories for each type of expense, such as "Groceries," "Utilities," "Transportation," and "Entertainment." Additionally, list your debts, including credit card balances, loans, and any other outstanding obligations.

Step 3: Fill in the Template

Income

In your budget template, enter your various sources of income. Specify the expected amount for each source and categorize it if necessary (e.g., "Salary," "Side Hustle," "Bonus," or "Investments").

Fixed Expenses

List your fixed expenses, including the amount and due date for each. Make sure to cover necessities like housing, utilities, transportation, and insurance.

Variable Expenses

Create budget categories for your variable expenses, and allocate a monthly amount to each one. Refer to past financial records or estimates for these amounts.

Savings and Goals

Dedicate a portion of your income to savings, investments, and financial goals. Common categories include an emergency fund, retirement savings, and specific goals like a vacation fund.

Debts

Include your debt payments as an expense category. Note the minimum monthly payments and the total outstanding balances.

Step 4: Calculate Totals

Sum up all your sources of income to calculate your total monthly income. Total your expenses by category to know the exact amount you are spending on each. Lastly, calculate the total amount you're allocating to savings and paying toward debt each month. Most templates have simple formulas you can use to get these totals. For instance, in Excel, you can just highlight the column with the category whose total you want and click "Autosum" to get the result. If you want to edit a particular amount, you don't have to manually calculate it from scratch, as the total will automatically adjust.

Step 5: Review and Adjust

Compare Income and Expenses

Compare your total income to your total expenses. Ideally, your income should exceed your expenses, leaving room for savings and debt repayment. If not, you may need to adjust your spending or consider finding additional sources of income.

Identify Areas for Improvement

Analyze your budget to identify areas where you can cut costs or allocate more funds. For example, if you are overspending in one category, reduce spending in another to balance your budget.

Set and Monitor Goals

Establish financial goals within your budget, such as saving for a vacation or paying off a credit card. Finally, track your progress regularly.

Homeownership requires a serious financial setup because it entails a lot of responsibilities. Unlike renting, where most expenses and responsibilities fall on the landlord, ownership shifts them to you. Budgeting for current and upcoming expenses will give you a sense of control and make homeownership less daunting for you.

Action Steps

Step 1: Understand Your Housing Expenses

❑ Explain mortgage types and how the payments are different.
❑ What are housing-related costs plus common repairs costs and how should they fit into your budget?
❑ Determine your Housing Expense Ratio and its significance.

Step 2: Build a Realistic Budget

❑ Gather financial information.
❑ Organize your income and expenses.
❑ Choose or create a budget template.

Step 3: Fill in the Budget Template and Review

❑ Input details into the chosen budget template, including mortgage payments, housing-related costs, and maintenance expenses.
❑ Calculate totals for each category.
❑ Make necessary adjustments to align with your financial goals.

Let's move forward. The next chapter will shed more light on what the real estate market entails.

4

UNDERSTANDING THE REAL ESTATE MARKET

Real estate cannot be lost or stolen, nor can it be carried away. Purchased with common sense, paid for in full, and managed with reasonable care, it is about the safest investment in the world.

— FRANKLIN D. ROOSEVELT

There are two types of housing market conditions you will encounter: the buyer's and the seller's markets. In the buyer's market, buyers have more options to choose from because the market is saturated with more properties available for sale than there are potential buyers. This means that you have an upper hand and more bargaining power when buying in this market because there are a multitude of favorable conditions, including low prices and higher inventory.

The opposite is true for the seller's market, as there are more buyers and fewer sellers. This means prices are higher and there is limited time to make your offer as housing options are few. You must understand the type of market you are in during your house-hunting quest.

KNOW WHAT YOU CAN AND CAN'T CONTROL

It is important to understand that you have no control over the prevailing market. However, you can control your actions and how you deal with the scenario. If you are buying in a buyer's market, chances are you will find your ideal home within your budget or even at a steal price with great negotiation. If getting your perfect home is not an urgent matter, you can research the real estate market to determine if it is ideal or not. You can always wait for conditions to be more favorable for you. However, if you are in a hurry to settle down, you must understand that you cannot control the prices in a hot market.

In fact, you might even have to pay more to make your offer more appealing than that of other buyers. Additionally, you can control how long you take before making an offer in the buyer's market, while time is of the essence in the seller's market. You must understand when you can control time and price because these fluctuate depending on the prevailing market.

HOW STRONG IS THE MARKET?

You must be proactive and assess the real estate market in your area of interest. If you drive around your potential location, you may start seeing an increase or decrease in the number of "for sale" signs. While this can be a determining factor in the pulse of the market, you have to widen your search and look at other sources. Check online listings and compare prices with previous months. Besides your local listings, the NAR publishes a monthly report for the latest home sales in the top 300 cities in the US (Bundrick, 2016). The report also indicates the duration of listings and the median asking prices, which you can study to determine the market trend.

CONDUCT A COMPARATIVE MARKET ANALYSIS

Whether you get the help of a real estate agent or go through popular websites like Zillow and Redfin, you can investigate how sale prices have been going for a particular property or similar ones in the same area. Investigating recent and comparable house sales will help give you an idea of how the market has been performing in that area.

KNOWLEDGE IS POWER

Knowing important details about home prices in your area of interest and how strong the market is puts you in an empowered position. You can effectively budget for your ideal home by searching within your means. You can also have an upper hand if you go house hunting with some background information you can use to negotiate better deals.

KEY FACTORS THAT AFFECT THE REAL ESTATE MARKET

The real estate market is influenced by a number of factors. Any dynamics in population, shift in the economy, fluctuation in interest rates, or changes in government policies can affect the price of homes or demand for certain property types. It is paramount that you are aware of these key factors so that you can make informed decisions regarding your home acquisition.

Demographics

Changes in the population, such as population growth, age distribution, and household size, can have a significant impact on housing demand. For example, an increase in young, first-time homebuyers can drive demand for starter homes and push prices up. Similarly, an aging population may create demand for retirement communities. Migration patterns, including urbanization, counterurbanization, or suburbanization, also affect housing markets. Therefore, you must pay attention to the national and regional population dynamics, as they may have a lasting effect on the real estate market.

The Economy

Economic factors have a direct impact on the real estate market. Economic indicators like employment rates, income levels, and consumer confidence influence the ability and willingness of individuals to buy and invest in real estate. In a strong economy, people are more likely to buy homes, invest in real estate, and start businesses, boosting the demand for commercial properties. In a weak economy, when employment rates and incomes are low, it becomes more difficult for people to afford housing. This may cause a drop in demand for houses, which can lead to sellers being forced to reduce their prices.

Interest Rates

Mortgage interest rates significantly influence the real estate market. When interest rates are low, borrowing is more affordable, making homeownership more accessible and driving demand for homes. Conversely, higher interest rates can deter potential buyers and investors, reducing demand and potentially cooling the market. Being aware of the direction of interest rates can also prepare you, as it indicates an impending season. You can expect a market shift based on whether interest rates have been dropping or rising for a certain period. They cannot drop or rise forever; a balance has to be maintained at some point.

Government Policies and Subsidies

The government has a way of boosting demand for real estate and improving the economy at large. Changes in government policies, such as tax laws and housing incentives, can alter real estate market dynamics. In a weak economy, the government may introduce tax incentives for qualifying homebuyers to boost sales. Additionally, government actions, such as infrastructure investment and development projects, can influence property values and demand in specific areas. These are some of the factors that have a direct or indirect effect on the real estate market.

REAL ESTATE MARKET ANALYSIS

Real estate market analysis, also known as comparative market analysis, is the process of evaluating and understanding the current and future conditions of a specific real estate market, be it a local neighborhood, city, or region. It involves collecting and assessing data to make informed decisions about real estate investments, development, or purchasing decisions. Therefore, it is one of the most important exercises you must do prior to buying your home to better understand the market in general. Sellers also need to consider conducting a thorough comparative market analysis to influence their sales targets.

What Are the Reasons to Conduct an Analysis?

Secure Investment

Wise investors use real estate market analysis as the backbone upon which they base their investment decisions. Understanding the current and future market conditions can provide guidelines on the best time, location, and type of property to invest in. Conducting a thorough analysis is imperative for a secure investment for investors and homebuyers alike.

Location Selection

The analysis will reveal potential locations in which to invest. For instance, if investors know that a particular location has a growing job market or industrial growth, they can buy property before the prices go up. Location also determines the accessibility of a property and what to prepare for to avoid any unexpected mishaps. An area with a reliable transportation network will attract more people than one that can only be reached by private transport. Moreover, a disaster-prone location is a risky investment that may come with high insurance costs. As a homebuyer, you want an accessible location with amenities that meet your needs, such as proximity to good schools, hospitals, and stores.

Development Projects

Similar to location selection, knowing if there are any scheduled developments around an area can help you and other investors know how these projects will affect the real estate market and the value of the properties. Doing an analysis means finding out if there are any infrastructure plans and evaluating their impact before investing in a property.

Property Valuation

Real estate market analysis determines the value of a property. The reasons above play a role in the price of a home. Therefore, assessing the market conditions, property location, development projects, demographics, and economic outlook all determine if your home will grow or drop in value. You must know this information before making a purchase, which is why you must do an analysis.

Tips for Conducting Effective Real Estate Market Analysis

Define Your Goals

Clarify the purpose of your analysis. Are you evaluating an investment opportunity, determining rental rates, or making a purchase decision? Your goals will guide the analysis. As a homebuyer, the main things you focus on may differ from the ones investors look for. For instance, a single-family home in a safe neighborhood with good schools, entertainment places, recreational parks, and access to hospitals might appeal to Terrence and Martha, first-time homebuyers with children. The same home might not fit a young, private couple that wants a secluded, picturesque gem to match their Instagram lifestyle.

Analyze the Property

Analyze the condition of the property and compare it with similar properties in the same area. You can identify comparable properties by their equivalent price, size, or type and evaluate your potential property based on that information. Collect this comprehensive data from any available source and narrow down your search as you get closer to what fits your goals. Someone looking for a fixer-upper may compare how much remodeling work a property will need compared to other distressed properties. This will also determine the price range they are willing to accept to compensate for the amount of work to be done, taking into account potential problems that might arise later.

Decide on the Market Value

After conducting all your analysis and researching how potential homes compare, you must now have a figure in mind. Bearing in mind that you do not have control over the pricing of any property, you can, however, decide on the price range you want to secure your property at. Having a target price in mind will help you refine your search, prioritize factors that may impact the property's value, and avoid surprises.

Steps for Conducting Real Estate Market Analysis

Study the Evolving Market

Take time to assess the overall performance of the global real estate market. This will indicate how it has evolved over the years. And as is common knowledge, real estate has been on the rise for centuries. Although its exponential rate has cooled down in the last few decades, the sentiment remains the same: It is a growing industry. To refine your study, ask the right questions regarding market volume, current trends, performance in terms of turnover, customers, and quantity of sales. Moreover, study the available products and services on the market and check who your competitors are.

Using multiple sources helps you avoid unbiased data. The FHA, NAR, Zillow Group, and Wall Street Journal are some of the resourceful mediums through which you can access this information. The National Association of Real Estate Brokers also has economists and analysts offering live commentary on the real estate market.

Study the Demand

Check the demand in the real estate market by studying who the major property buyers are and what their typical behavior is. Study the types of property most people buy and analyze how much they often spend on their purchases. Study the factors that contribute to the demand, such as job opportunities, amenities, and schools. Look into any demographic trends that suggest increasing or decreasing demand.

Narrow Your Search to Your Target Areas

Focusing on your preferred amenities and needs, use the strategy you used to study the general market and narrow down your search. Street View by Google Maps and your local websites can provide comprehensive data specific to your target neighborhood.

The Environmental and Legal Study

Assess the environmental factors affecting the area, such as proximity to parks and noise levels. Review local zoning laws and regulations that may impact property use. Finally, check for any legal issues or restrictions related to the property. The county clerk's office, local planning department, and official municipal website provide zoning maps that display zoning designations, codes, and related documents.

Study the Offers

Analyze the inventory of homes available for sale and their prices. Consider the types of properties available and look into the average time they stay on the market. This will help you structure your offer to have a competitive edge over other buyers, especially if properties sell like hotcakes.

Create a Comprehensive Report

Summarize your findings in a clear and organized report. Include data on property values, market trends, demand, and supply. Provide insights into the environmental and legal aspects affecting the area.

Understanding the market is a complicated and serious business. If all of the prior suggestions for this analysis seem overwhelming, do what millions of people do everyday: find a great real estate agent and use their expertise to accomplish the same goal. Their job is to understand the market and find the best house for you.

TREND PREDICTIONS

The real estate market is constantly evolving, and the following trends are shaping the way people search for and purchase homes. Understanding these trends can help you make informed decisions about your own home search.

House Hunting Will Go Digital

Technology is transforming how people do business, including buying and selling homes. Virtual tours, online listings, and digital platforms are making it easier than ever to find and view properties without ever leaving your home. This trend is likely to continue, and it will be increasingly important for buyers and sellers to be comfortable using technology to navigate the real estate market.

People Are Likely to Move From Cities to Suburbs

The COVID-19 pandemic has led many people to reassess their priorities and lifestyle choices. As a result, we are seeing a trend of people moving from densely populated cities to more suburban or rural areas. The desire for more space, affordability, and a better quality of life are the driving forces behind this shift.

The Popularity of Sunbelts Will Continue to Rise

Sunbelt states, such as Florida, Texas, and Arizona, have long been popular destinations for retirees and families. This trend is likely to continue, as these states offer warm weather, lower taxes, and a more relaxed lifestyle.

Home Prices Will Continue to Rise

Home prices have been rising steadily in recent years, and this trend is expected to continue. This is due to a number of factors, including low interest rates, strong demand, and a limited supply of homes.

Demand for Single-Family Homes Will Create Shortage

The demand for single-family homes is high, and this is putting upward pressure on prices. A number of factors perpetuate this, including millennials entering the homeownership market, an increase in the number of single-person households, and a preference for more space and privacy.

Mortgage Rates Are Likely to Rise

Although mortgage rates are currently low, they are expected to rise in the coming years. This could make it more expensive to buy a home, so it is important to lock in a low rate if you are planning to buy in the near future. It is also crucial to note that the FHA usually raises or drops interest rates to curb inflation. Therefore, mortgage rate fluctuations are dependent on overall inflation and what the government does to keep things under control.

Rental Property Market Will Decline

The rental property market is expected to decline in the coming years. This is due to a number of factors, including the increase in homeownership, the shift to suburban living, and the decline in the number of young adults living in cities.

POPULAR PROPERTIES AVAILABLE IN THE UNITED STATES

There is a wide range of property types to choose from when buying a home. They usually vary in size, location, and lifestyle preference. From offering privacy to shared living with communal amenities, your choice will be influenced by your budget and personal needs. Private properties may come with high maintenance costs, yet they offer the freedom to do as you please with no restrictions. Alternatively, shared properties may be cost-savvy but restrictive and lack privacy.

Single-Family Homes

Single-family homes are standalone, detached houses designed to accommodate one family, like yours as a first-time homebuyer. They are highly sought-after for their privacy and space, often featuring a yard or outdoor area. They are ideal for families and individuals seeking independence and a sense of ownership.

Semidetached Homes

Semidetached homes, also known as duplexes, or patio homes, are two homes that share a common wall, even though they are owned by different individuals or families. They offer a balance between the independence of a single-family home and the cost-sharing benefits of multifamily properties.

Multifamily Homes

Multifamily homes are properties that can accommodate multiple families or individuals in separate units. This category includes duplexes, triplexes, quadplexes, and apartment buildings. Investors often choose multifamily properties for rental income. You can also opt for a multifamily home if you are looking for a home with shared amenities to save money. You must bear in mind that these are often governed by the HOA, which comes with a lot of restrictions, like pet ownership.

Townhomes

Townhomes are typically multilevel properties that share walls with neighboring units but have individual entrances. They offer a blend of single-family and apartment living, combining the privacy of a house with the convenience of shared maintenance in a planned community. Generally, they are not governed by an HOA, however, there are exceptions to that rule. As I write, I am sitting in my home office in my townhome and my community of townhomes are governed by an HOA.

Apartments

Apartments are typically part of larger residential buildings and are available for rent. They are an attractive choice for individuals or families who prefer renting and living in urban or suburban areas. Apartments offer a wide range of sizes and amenities, such as a communal pool, tennis court, or gymnasium.

Condominiums

Similar to apartments in structure, being part of a building or complex, condominiums offer a combination of urban living and ownership. Condo owners share common spaces and amenities but have ownership rights to their specific units. Condos are popular in urban areas and may offer added conveniences like security and maintenance. They are also subject to HOA fees and regulations.

Co-Ops

Co-ops involve residents who jointly own and manage the entire property. When you buy into a co-op, you become a shareholder in the cooperative corporation, granting you the right to live in one of the units. Co-ops often have more stringent ownership and management requirements than condos.

Tiny Homes

As the name hints, tiny homes are small, compact houses, often with a minimalist design, intended to reduce living space and expenses. They are gaining popularity among individuals, such as young couples and empty-nesters, looking to downsize, live more sustainably, or achieve financial freedom.

Manufactured Homes

Manufactured homes, also commonly referred to as mobile homes or trailers, are prefabricated residential structures that are constructed in a factory and then transported to their final location for installation. These homes are built to meet national construction and safety standards, making them a cost-effective housing option for many people. Because they can be moved intact to another plot of land, manufactured homes are considered personal property (chattel), sort of like a recreational vehicle.

Modular Homes

Modular homes are built in a factory and then assembled on site and anchored to a foundation. Since they become immovable, they are considered real property just like a house fully constructed on site.

HOW TO SELECT YOUR HOME

Location is usually a priority for most first-time buyers. Ideally, you want a house that makes your daily commute easier. If you are traveling to work or your kids are commuting to school, the place must be close to a transportation network and within a reasonable distance. You can compromise on many things, but location is not one of them. You have to love the neighborhood because you are going to spend a long time in this location. Location is also going to determine the future value of your property. A home situated in an area with growing opportunities will increase in value, while one in an inaccessible area might not increase much.

Buy for Your Lifestyle

A house with a big, state-of-the-art kitchen might appeal to a master chef ready to prepare gourmet meals, while a simple house with picturesque views could be any artist's dream. Your perfect home will have to fit your lifestyle and be within your financial means. If you do not want to sell the farm or other large asset in order to afford your first home, you may consider buying an undervalued property whose potential is yet to be realized. If you are up for a challenge and want to get your hands dirty to customize your home, a distressed property might also be an option, as it will be relatively affordable and in need of a few touch-ups where you can give it character. You just have to be prepared to spend some money and effort to make it a habitable space before you move in, meaning this is only an option if you are not in any hurry to settle into your home.

Consider Your Financial Means

To get a loan for your dream home, you need to follow the rules set by the lender. This means you have to meet their requirements. It's really important to think about how much money you can put towards buying your home. This includes the initial payment and the money you'll pay every month. You can use your savings, grants from the government or local organizations, loans from the government, loans from private companies, or different types of mortgages to help you afford it. It's also important to try and reduce any money you owe so that you can comfortably pay your monthly mortgage and insurance. Plus, it's a good idea to have some money saved for unexpected things that might come up. Lenders like it when you have extra money saved because it shows them that you're prepared for any problems and can handle them, which makes them more likely to lend you money for your home.

Think Long-Term

A house is a long-term investment. As I mentioned earlier, this is where you will probably start your family and create lifetime memories. Therefore, you'll need to think ahead when considering the location, neighborhood, and community because once you've bought, you cannot easily change any of these. While you can custom-make your house through renovations and redesign your yard, that's about all you can change. Consider things like the climate of an area, and be prepared to spend money on either cooling or heating systems in the long run. Select your home knowing what you can and cannot control over time.

Resolve Conflicting House Visions

For most people, buying a home affects more than one person. People living together may have different visions or conflicting ideas for their shared dream home, often causing squabbles and relationship rifts. Even single parents need to consider their children's needs and coparenting schedules when deciding on a permanent home. Therefore, it's crucial to be open and have clear communication regarding what is best for everyone involved.

While it might be impossible for everyone to get what they want, some compromises can be made to make this near-lifetime decision a win for everyone. You can even make this easier by laying out your desires way before you begin house hunting so that you factor them into your joint search. Discuss what amenities matter most and the nonnegotiables, then strike a balance wherever possible.

Understanding the real estate market means knowing what drives home prices in different seasons so that you buy when terms are more favorable for buying. It also depends on the type, size, and condition of the property. Knowing some trend predictions also helps you prepare for action by knowing the direction of the market in time and deciding where to buy.

Action Steps

❏ Analyze the Local Market by studying recent property sales in your desired area to understand pricing trends and property demand.
❏ Use this data to set realistic expectations for your own property transactions.
❏ Keep track of factors like demographics, economy,

interest rates, and government policies. Stay updated on economic indicators and mortgage rates to adapt your real estate plans.

❑ Make educated guesses about upcoming real estate trends, like digital house hunting and shifts in housing preferences, then see how these trends might affect your property decisions and plan accordingly.

❑ Select a property based on your lifestyle needs, budget, and long-term goals.

❑ Have open discussions with others involved in the decision to resolve any conflicting preferences and find a suitable choice together.

Moving on - the next chapter is your guide to a successful journey, as it focuses on teaching you exactly what to do to position yourself for better deals.

5

YOUR GUIDE TO SUCCESS

W ith more than 50% of Americans having no idea what a mortgage is and lacking information regarding the housing market (Melore, 2022), it is apparent that this group will likely not do anything about improving their financial position. Getting preapproved for this home loan requires one to have a stable and reliable income, manage debt well, improve their credit score, and keep their expenses in check. This chapter will shed more light on how to gear up for success in homeownership by defining the prequalification and preapproval processes to help you avoid biting off more than you can chew and to choose the right financing for your home.

MORTGAGE PREAPPROVAL

A mortgage preapproval is a preliminary loan estimate lenders give you after assessing your relevant documents, such as your proof of a stable source of income and credit history. When submitting these documents, you will fill out a mortgage application, and the lender will verify your documents and perform a credit check to verify your creditworthiness. Within a few days— up to 10 working days—you will get a preapproval letter that you can use to appeal to buyers with an offer to purchase a home because it indicates that you are able to secure a mortgage.

The Importance of Being Preapproved

Advantage Over Other Buyers

Approaching sellers with your desire to buy a home is usually a competitive process because other buyers are out there hoping to be the one who buys the house. However, if you are already preapproved, you appear as a more serious buyer and have a better chance with the seller. It indicates that you already have the financial means to afford the house, rather than someone who could just be asking for because they're curious.

You Will Borrow Within Your Means

A mortgage preapproval shows the maximum of the loan for which you qualify. Therefore, when you shop for a house, you are already looking for one within your financial means. You can then plan your finances without overcommitting. And no one says you have to buy a house at the top of your spending limit; you can still chose a house you love that is selling for a lower amount that fits your financial goals.

Preapproval vs. Prequalification

So, what's the difference? Most people confuse a mortgage preapproval with a mortgage prequalification. A prequal simply is an estimate of how much you can qualify for, while the preapproval is an offer, but not a commitment, to lend you a certain amount of money valid for up to 90 days. It takes a few hours to get a prequalification because the lender requires fewer details than they require with a preapproval.

You can apply for prequalification online by just providing a few details about your income, basic information about your bank accounts, credit check, down payment, and desired mortgage amount. With a preapproval, you have to also provide supporting documents like your recent bank statements, copies of pay stubs to prove income and signed tax returns from the past 2 years. A preapproval is not a guarantee that the lender agrees to give you a loan; you can still be denied a loan after being preapproved. Even the terms of the loan might change when it comes to the actual loan.

Unlike an approved loan, a preapproved loan does not hurt your credit score. Getting a preapproval at least a year ahead of your home purchase allows you to know how much you can afford and start looking for houses within that budget. Just remember you'll need a recent preapproval closer to the date of making an offer to purchase.

Preapproval Steps

Determine Your Monthly Payment

Before you start talking to lenders, it's good to have a figure in mind of how much you want to spend monthly on a home. You can then use the mortgage calculator as instructed previously to narrow down the amount you might qualify for. Knowing how much you want to spend monthly will ensure that you stick to your budget even when a lender offers you a higher loan amount.

Find a Mortgage Preapproval Company

There are several mortgage companies you can approach for a mortgage preapproval. You can even visit NerdWallet, Rocket Mortgage, or Homebuyer websites and fill out a mortgage application online. Remember that you do not have to go through with any loan application after the preapproval stage. Many people end up using a different mortgage company to get the final loan, not specifically the one that approved them.

Gather Your Financial Documents

To go forward with your application, lenders will require you to provide financial documentation to prove your income and run a credit check on you. Have your bank statements, W-2 statements, tax returns, pay stubs, and proof of deposits, as well as student loan statements or any debt information you have. While you may not need to upload these documents right away, it's smart to keep them nearby for when you are asked to provide them.

Get Preapproved

An online self-service application can take as little as 3 minutes to determine if you will get approved or not. As I mentioned, getting the preapproval letter can take up to 10 working days, although most companies strive to respond on the same day.

DIFFERENT TYPES OF MORTGAGES

Depending on your financial needs and your available resources, there are several types of financing to help you make your home-buying dream a reality. These mortgages mainly differ in terms of qualification criteria and the type of property you are financing. It is important to know what each loan requires and what the pros and cons of each are so that you can financially plan for the one that meets your needs.

Conventional Loan

A conventional mortgage, also known as a traditional loan, is one offered by private institutions like banks and credit unions. This means that it is not government-insured, making it riskier for lenders. One of the major upsides of conventional loans is that they often offer relatively competitive interest rates and longer lending periods to qualifying borrowers. Based on November 2023 figures, you can expect to pay around 6.5% or 7.26% interest on your mortgage over a 15- or 30-year period, respectively (Getler, 2023).

However, the downsides of conventional loans are that they usually require large down payments and near-perfect credit scores, strict criteria that are often difficult for first-timers. For instance, you must have a credit score of at least 680, and the interest rate will depend on the size of your down payment. If you're not putting down at least a 20% deposit, a conventional loan will also require you to have PMI.

Real-life scenario:

Meet Mark, a recent college graduate who landed his dream job in the city and wants to own his own home.

Mark visits a local bank and inquires about a conventional mortgage to buy his first house. The loan officer explains that while conventional loans offer competitive rates and longer repayment schedules, they also require sizable down payments and excellent credit scores.

Despite Mark's stable income from his new job, he's concerned about the hefty down payment. The loan officer informs him that a down payment of at least 20% is preferred to avoid PMI, which adds to the cost of the loan.

Also, Mark's credit score took a hit while he was in college and missed making some credit card payments so his credit score is below 680, the required amount for lower interest rates. The loan officer explains Mark will have to pay higher rates.

Faced with the tight criteria and the cost of the down payment, Mark realizes he will either have to wait to buy or explore other loan options. Mark finds guidance from a financial advisor to better understand his options and learn how he can improve his credit score. Whether he ends up with a conventional loan or other financing, a better credit score will improve his odds of getting a loan.

Fixed-Rate Mortgage

An FRM is a home loan with an interest rate that doesn't change over the course of the lending period. This means if the loan is for 15 or 30 years, you will pay the same interest rate for the entire period, without fluctuations. The predictable monthly payments make it easy to make a long-term budget. The disadvantage of an FRM is that the initial payments can be high compared to those of an ARM. The best thing to do with either the FRM or the ARM is determine what payment you can afford at the beginning and also look at the picture to see how much you will pay for the rest of the lending period. Knowing both these facts can help you make a better decision, which should give you peace of mind and a sense of control.

Even though you choose a FRM, you always have the option to refinance the mortgage if you want a lower rate later. It's important to note that the monthly payments that remain unchanged for the duration of the loan are only limited to the principal and interest, excluding other expenses like property taxes and homeowners insurance. Both property taxes and homeowners insurance are at the whim of the market, so they often increase over time, no matter what your loan type.

Adjustable-Rate Mortgage

An ARM starts off low and changes depending on current market interest rate trends. This means that the introductory rates are lower for a fixed period and fluctuate for the remainder of the lending period, depending on economic conditions. For instance, a 5/6 ARM means you will pay a fixed, lower interest rate for the first 5 years and then a variable rate that changes every 6 months thereafter. If the rate increases, this means your monthly mortgage will increase as well, and the opposite applies if the rate declines.

It can be deceiving when you start out with an interest rate that makes your payments easy to afford if you forget that the rate will change and those payments will go up. Plus, it makes it really hard to budget as the later payments fluctuate and they may be quite high as the economy changes. The risk of high ongoing monthly payments is the reason some people might prefer locking in a fixed rate instead. An ARM is perfect for individuals who do not plan to stay long-term in the financed property and want to pay less while they're in the home. However, borrowers risk paying higher interest rates if they are still living there when the lower interest rate term ends.

Jumbo Loan

As the name suggests, a jumbo loan is a big loan that exceeds the conforming borrowing limit set by the FHA. Because it is not insured by the government, it is considered a high-risk loan. Therefore, it carries strict qualification criteria, including credit scores over 700 and large down payments of around 10% and 20%. Jumbo loans are not common with first-time homebuyers because they are typically used to finance expensive properties worth more than $726,200 or $1,089,300 in higher-cost areas (Dehan, 2023b).

Government-Insured Loans

This is the easiest path for most first-time home buyers: government-backed loans are common financing options geared toward first-time homeowners with limited resources and poor credit scores. Unlike conventional mortgages, these loans make it fairly easy to finance a home, even with a low or no down payment. There are three common government-backed loans you can apply for: FHA, Veteran Affairs (VA), and the United States Department of Agriculture (USDA) loans.

FHA Loan

FHA-approved loans have varying fees depending on whether you are applying through the bank, credit union, mortgage broker, or mortgage banker. You can qualify for an FHA-backed loan with a credit score as low as 580 and a down payment of 3.5%, or a 500 score if you put down a 10% deposit (Dehan, 2023b). While they offer relatively low interest rates and are accessible to homeowners with less-than-perfect credit scores at low down payments, FHA loans have a condition of upfront and monthly MIPs. The eligibility criteria include the DTI ratio and the condition of the property being financed.

Many buyers, in the same situation as our friend, Mark, who was researching the conventional loan, likely end up here: getting an FHA loan. They don't have to wait to save up that large deposit and their lower credit scores don't keep they from entering the world of homeownership.

VA Loan

Calling all veterans - since you were willing to put yourself at risk in defending our country, this is one of the benefits of your service. Backed by the US. Department of Veteran Affairs, VA mortgages are another financing option reserved for eligible veterans, service members, and surviving spouses. Once you provide evidence that you or your spouse served on active duty for at least 90 days or were released under honorable conditions, you can qualify for this loan. Some of the great benefits offered by VA loans include 100% financing—no down payment required—low interest rates, and no PMI. If you want to know more specific details on VA loans, you can find them on the VA website (Marquand & Getler, 2023).

USDA Loan

If you are buying property in a rural area and your household income meets the criteria, you can qualify for a 100%-backed USDA loan that requires no down payment and comes with competitive interest rates. The main conditions include the location of the property and the income limit. Ideally, the limits are $110,650 and $146,050 per household of 1–4 and 5–8 members, respectively (Neighbors Bank, 2023). Additionally, there are other state and local government programs that you can inquire about in your region. While they may vary in qualification criteria, these programs usually cater to homebuyers with limited resources and offer favorable interest rates as well as down payment assistance.

102 | V J DEAN

Other Types of Loans

Balloon Mortgages

A balloon mortgage is one that starts very low in the first few years and ends with a large payment at the end of the lending period. Essentially, the rate you pay at the beginning is based on a 30-year term, even though you only pay for a short period, such as 7 years. You must be prepared to pay the remainder as a lump sum when the term ends. A balloon mortgage is ideal for investors who can generate money during their lending period so that they can settle the outstanding balance. If you're not in a job or industry that guarantees you'll generate a large pay-day income, it's best to look at other loan options, as a huge balloon payment would only cause trouble for most new homeowners.

Construction Loans

If you decide to build a house instead of buying one, there is the option of a construction loan. A construction loan is typically a short-term financing option ideal for borrowers who can pay a large down payment and prove their eligibility to cover the monthly payments.

Interest-Only Loans

An interest-only loan is one where the borrower initially pays interest only in the first years of the loan term and only pays principal and interest later. During the time when the borrower is paying only the interest, the loan balance remains the same; therefore, it is ideal for people not looking to build equity in a home. After the interest-only term ends, which is typically 5–10 years, the loan converts to a traditional loan where both the principal and interest must be paid for the remaining lending period.

Piggyback Loans

A piggyback loan, also known as an 80-10-10 loan, is a type of mortgage that involves taking out 2 loans simultaneously to avoid paying PMI and making a smaller down payment. The 1st loan covers 80% of the home purchase, the 2nd loan (piggyback loan) covers 10% of the down payment, and the borrower comes up with the remaining 10% to make it 20%.

These loans can also be known as home equity lines of credit (HELOC) and/or a bridge loan. With both the purchase loan and the second loan, the house is used as collateral to secure the loans.

You can see from all these loan options that there are resources out there for almost every borrowing situation. You just need to study the options and work with lenders to find the one best suited to your home buying situation.

IMPROVING YOUR CREDIT SCORE

One thing that most lenders focus on when lending money is the borrower's credit score. This important financial metric evaluates your financial responsibility based on your credit history. Having a high credit score can increase your chances of getting a loan at better interest rates, while a poor credit score will hurt your chances of financing. You can know your credit score by pulling your record from the three national credit bureaus: Experian, Equifax, and TransUnion. Knowing your credit score is the first step toward improving it.

Why Does a Good Credit Score Matter?

A credit score is a measure of your ability to use credit responsibility, and your credit report shows how you handle credit by looking at when you use credit and if you pay on time. Your report ranges between 300 and 850, with an excellent score being above 760 and a poor one being below 620. Lenders use it to determine whether on not you are likely to pay back your loans and whether or not you will pay on time. A lower score means you are a high-risk borrower who might default. Lenders want to loan to responsible people and that might not be you if you don't use credit wisely. If your score is low and a lender does decide to loan to you, they charge a high interest rate to make up for the risk they are taking.

Conventional lenders usually require you to have a credit score of 680 or above. If you have anything below that, you can expect to pay higher interest on your mortgage, higher down payment requirements, PMI, or rejection. Still, as we discussed before, you can qualify for FHA-approved mortgages even if your credit score is 580 (Araj, 2023).

Ways to Build a Good Credit Score

Review Your Credit Reports

You cannot address any issues you don't know about, so the first step is to pull your credit reports and see what they show. You must monitor where you are making poor decisions and work from there to change how you handle credit. You are entitled to request a free report from the credit bureaus I mentioned. This should be done on a regular basis until you have a good credit score. Check your reports carefully for fraud or errors and dispute them immediately.

Pay Your Bills on Time

Your credit payment history makes up 35% of your credit score, making it the most important area to fix. When looking at your report, you will see areas where you skipped or delayed paying your credit. You must fix this by making on-time payments and never skip any payments in the future. You can do this by setting automatic payments from your bank or creating alerts on payment due dates so that you never miss a payment.

Limit Your Credit Utilization to 30% or Below

Your credit usage accounts for 30% of your credit score. Using more than 30% of your available credit is a red flag that paints you as an irresponsible spender. Meaning, if you have a credit limit of $6,000, you must only use $2,000 or less.

Keep Old Accounts and Limit New Credit Requests

A record of old accounts you are maintaining is another positive factor that adds 15% to your score. Don't close out old accounts, but keep them open even if you are no longer using them. The age of your account plays a role when lenders review your credit history. An old account, even if it was paid off, indicates a better record than a new account. Avoid applying for new credit.

Pad Out a Thin Credit File

A thin credit file simply means you have little to no credit history, so it can't generate a credit score. This happens if you have never had any debt, and it makes you seem inexperienced with credit to lenders. You can pad out your thin credit file using Experian

Boost, which gathers financial information that does not reflect on your credit report from your banking history and bill payments.

Another option to padding out your account is to apply for a credit card and use it like cash. In other words, the places where you normally pay cash, write a check, or use your debit card, you would use the credit card and pay the full bill when it comes due. That means you still aren't spending any more than the cash you have available, but you're now building a credit history record.

Become an Authorized User

If you have a friend or relative who has a high-limit credit card account with a good history, you can ask to be added as an authorized user, and this will go to your credit record. You can either agree to have access to the card and even make payments on it, or you can simply be listed as a user. This can have a high impact, especially if you have a thin credit file.

Have a Mixture of Credit

Spread your credit history around by having different types of accounts. Having a mix of credit cards and installment loans on your record can improve your score, as it shows lenders that you can manage debt responsibly.

Consider Debt Consolidation

If you have too many accounts that you can't handle, it is better to apply for a loan that will help you pay them off and leave you with one debt. Debt consolidation can also help you pay lower interest on one loan than on multiple accounts. Therefore, you will also pay down your debt more easily and fix your credit use ratio.

Monitor Your Progress

Use credit monitoring services to track your credit score over time. This is the easiest way to track changes in your credit score based on any financial activity, such as a paid-off account or a new credit application. Receiving alerts will help you know if your financial activity was positive or negative. You can even see if there is fraudulent activity on your profile that you must dispute immediately.

Working With a Credit Counselor

If you need help managing your credit, establishing a monthly budget, or overall getting hold of your finances, working with a credit counselor might be the way to go. Fortunately, there are a lot of free-to-use credit counseling agencies in the US. A credit counselor will save you more time while improving your situation because they will offer targeted advice to improve it.

DOCUMENTS REQUIRED FOR A MORTGAGE APPLICATION

When applying for a mortgage, there are important documents you must prepare, as lenders will request them. You will have to gather your documents as soon as you are about to apply for a mortgage and organize them into an application folder for easy access when you have to upload them.

Mortgage Application Information

You will need to fill out a mortgage application form called the Uniform Residential Loan Application, which typically requires you to declare your financial details. This form acts as the cover letter of your application; therefore, you must be as truthful as possible when you fill it out because lenders use this form to determine your eligibility before checking your supporting documents. You can find this form on any mortgage company website or at their offices if you are doing an in-person application.

Income Verification

The second most important piece of information lenders will require is your proof of income. You must declare all your sources of income, including your salary, spousal or child support, Social Security benefits, rental income if you have any, or any income from a side hustle. The lender will request that you submit at least 2 years of your tax returns. If you don't have copies, use IRS Form 4506-C to request copies. You will also need to provide your employer-signed pay stubs for the last 30 days along with your W-2 forms to verify how much you have earned from your income. If you're self-employed, then you'll need your 1099 forms.

Bank Statements and Other Assets

Lenders will request that you submit your bank statements, investment assets, retirement accounts, life insurance, or any other assets in your name. Besides your financial statements showing your income and usage, they will also show your reserves in case of an emergency, as well as prove that your down payment has been in your account for some time and has not miraculously appeared overnight. Moreover, your bank statements will reveal your DTI ratio, which we have established is an important metric in mortgage applications.

Credit Report

With your verbal and written permission, lenders will pull out your credit report from the credit bureaus to evaluate your credit score. Your credit score will determine the type of mortgage for which you qualify.

Other Records

You will also need to provide proof of identity to verify who you are. If you are getting financial help as a gift from a relative or friend, you will need to submit a signed agreement indicating that the money is not to be reimbursed. You may also be required to provide the donor's bank statement to prove their source of income. Furthermore, you must provide the sales or purchase agreement showing the amount of the home you're hoping to buy. You will also need to provide your rental history, as this will give lenders your rental payment information. On-time rental payments will look good on your application.

The main focus of this chapter was to position you for action in the homebuying process. Getting a preapproval requires meticulous financial records that clearly show your income stability and credit management. Once you meet the criteria, success is yours, and you can look forward to the next chapter in your life.

Action Steps

❏ Set your goal to get mortgage Preapproval for a mortgage from a lender. Clearly state the difference between preapproval and prequalification.

❏ Collect the needed documents and speak with a mortgage expert to begin the preapproval process.

❏ Learn about various mortgage types, like conventional loans, fixed-rate, adjustable-rate, jumbo loans, and government-insured loans. Which type fits your financial situation and goals?

❏ Improve your financial picture by boosting your credit score for a better chance of mortgage approval. This means paying bills on time and reducing debts, and if necessary, seek advice from a credit counselor.

❏ Gather mortgage application documents, including proof of income, bank statements, credit reports, and other relevant records.

Now, let's move on to the next chapter in the book, which is your guide to knowing what you want in a dream home.

MAKE A DIFFERENCE WITH YOUR HOME BUYING REVIEW

UNLOCK THE JOURNEY OF FINDING YOUR DREAM HOME

Buying Your First Home by V J Dean is a must-read for anyone stepping into the world of real estate. With a friendly and approachable style, V J Dean offers practical advice to make the daunting task of purchasing your first home a more manageable and informed journey.

Why Your Review Matters

Your insights and experiences are invaluable! By sharing your thoughts on *Buying Your First Home*, you help others navigate their own home-buying journey. Your review can provide guidance, reassurance, and the confidence others need to make informed decisions.

Writing Your Review: A Simple Guide

We love hearing your thoughts! When writing your review, consider the following:

✓ **Clarity and Honesty:** Be clear about what you loved and what you think could be improved.

Examples: Did a particular piece of advice stand out? Share how it impacted your home-buying process.

✓ **Recommendations:** Would you recommend this book to others? Who do you think would benefit most from reading it?

Remember: Your Words Have Impact

Just like how V J Dean advises not to let emotions override financial decisions in home buying, your balanced and thoughtful review can guide others towards making wise choices. Your words can be the beacon that lights the path for many first-time homebuyers.

Share Your Review Now

Ready to share your thoughts? Just scan the **QR CODE** below to submit your review.

To access the book, type this link into Google, then scroll to the bottom of the page to leave your review: https://a.co/d/4aOeilM

Your generosity in sharing your experience can make a significant difference in someone else's journey to buying their first home.

Thank you for contributing to our community of readers and future homeowners!

6

KNOW WHAT YOU WANT

The COVID-19-imposed lockdown made almost half of Americans regret their home purchases when the reality of their dwellings hit them. Since most people were spending less time at home pre-pandemic, their limited space or location was not a big deal until the only option they had was to find comfort in the same homes. Only then did people realize that there were a lot of features they disregarded during the homebuying process. Fortunately, this opened the eyes of people like you who are yet to buy their first homes. This chapter is about helping you decide what you must look for in a home based on your needs and wants. Knowing what you want will help you stick to your budget and avoid regretting your purchase.

IDENTIFYING MUST-HAVE FEATURES

While it is possible to custom-make your home to your liking or invest in some add-ons, it is important to know beforehand what distinct features you want in a home. Knowing what to look for in a property will help you narrow down your potential homes during your search. We know that different things matter to different people, so it is okay if you might have a slightly different opinion on any of the features below.

These are common must-have features most homebuyers seek, and you can fine-tune them according to your needs and desires. The ideal home is a reflection of your personal needs, wants, and lifestyle. Prioritize the features that matter most to you, and seek guidance from real estate professionals to find a property that meets your vision of a comfortable and fulfilling home.

Location

Location is the most important thing to decide on because moving your house, no matter how much you like the interior or exterior, is next to impossible. Oh, it's been done. I bet at some point in your life you saw that semi on the highway pulling a house on a huge flatbed, but that's rare due to the cost and hassle of preparing a new location with plumbing, electrical, land development, sewer, and all the things that you will find already in place when you find a home in your desired location.

The location of your home significantly impacts your daily life, commute times, access to amenities, and overall quality of life. Consider factors like closeness to work, schools, parks, shopping centers, and cultural attractions.

Square Footage

The size of your home should accommodate your current and future needs. Consider your family size, the number of guests you typically host, and the amount of living space you require for comfort and functionality. You must bear in mind that the bigger the size, the more responsibilities there are: utilities, maintenance, and upkeep.

Outdoor Area

If you enjoy outdoor activities or have pets, a yard or outdoor space is a valuable asset. Your children and pets can roam freely in your yard and explore the outdoors. Consider the size and layout of the yard, the presence of patios or decks, and the potential for landscaping or gardening.

Number of Bedrooms and Bathrooms

The number of bedrooms and bathrooms is crucial for accommodating your family size and guests. Consider the number of occupants, the need for separate spaces for children or work-from-home arrangements, and the availability of en suite bathrooms.

Kitchen Layout and Features

The kitchen is the heart of the home, so its layout and features should align with your cooking style and preferences. Consider the counter space, storage options, appliance placement, natural light, and overall functionality. The person who loves creating scrumptious meals from scratch may value a bigger open-plan kitchen with a gas stove, an oven, and a dining area to entertain family or guests while cooking. Someone who spends less time in the kitchen may prefer to go with a basic layout.

Living Area

The size of the living area also depends on the size of your household and your desire to invite family and friends over. You may also want more than one living room or great room if you have kids so that they have their own TV and space separate from where adults hang out.

The Age and Style of a Home

The age and style of the home influence its visual appeal and potential maintenance requirements. Consider your preferences for modern or traditional architecture, the condition of older homes, and the potential for remodeling or renovation.

Garage

A garage provides secure parking for your vehicle, storage space for belongings, and a potential workspace for hobbies or projects. Consider the size of the garage, the presence of more parking spaces, and the possibility of converting it into a living area.

Extra Space

A flex space, such as a loft, bonus room, or finished basement, provides versatility and adaptability to your changing needs. It can serve as a home office, playroom, guest room, or additional living area.

Allowance to Upgrade Features

If you can see yourself making future expansions or modifications, consider the potential for adding a room, expanding a living area, or constructing a deck or patio. Check for zoning regulations and neighborhood restrictions.

Things to Look for When Buying a Home

Home Exterior

Inspect the roof for signs of damage, such as missing shingles, loose or damaged flashing, or sagging or uneven surfaces. Check for cracks, dents, or warping in the siding. Ensure the paint or exterior finish is in good condition and not peeling or bubbling. Examine windows and doors for cracks, gaps, or loose seals. Check that they open and close smoothly and securely. Inspect the foundation for cracks, bowing, or signs of water damage. Check that gutters and downspouts are clear of debris and functioning properly to direct water away from the house.

Living Room

Inspect walls and ceilings for cracks, water stains, or signs of mold or mildew. Check for proper insulation and adequate ventilation. Examine the flooring for scratches, dents, or signs of moisture damage. Ensure the flooring is level and secure. Check windows for cracks, gaps, or loose seals. Test their operation to ensure they open and close smoothly.

HVAC

Inspect the HVAC system for signs of wear and tear, leaks, or rust. Check the condition of filters, ducts, and vents. Test the thermostat to ensure it is functioning correctly and regulating the temperature effectively. Check that air circulation is adequate throughout the house, especially in areas with limited ventilation.

Attic

Inspect the attic for signs of structural damage, such as sagging beams or cracked rafters. Check the condition of the insulation to ensure it is providing adequate thermal protection. Ensure proper ventilation in the attic to prevent moisture buildup and promote air circulation.

Basement

Inspect for signs of moisture, such as dampness, water stains, or mold growth in the basement. Check for proper drainage and waterproofing. Examine the basement walls and floors for cracks, bowing, or signs of structural damage. Ensure adequate lighting and ventilation in the basement to prevent moisture buildup and promote a healthy environment.

Garage

Check that garage doors and openings are functioning properly and securely. Examine the garage flooring for cracks, dents, or signs of moisture damage. Ensure adequate lighting in the garage to enhance visibility and safety.

Power Outlets

Verify that electrical outlets and switches are functioning properly and securely mounted because poorly placed outlets will limit your layout choices. Verify that there are sufficient electrical outlets in each room and convenient locations. Inspect outlets for signs of damage, loose connections, or improper grounding. Test their functionality by plugging in appliances. Ensure that ground-fault circuit interrupters are installed in areas where there is moisture, such as bathrooms and kitchens. Inspect the electrical panel for signs of damage, loose connections, or overloaded circuits.

DISTINGUISHING BETWEEN NEEDS AND WANTS

When embarking on the journey of homeownership, it is crucial to decide which are essential needs and which are your desired wants. This distinction will guide your search, helping you prioritize the features that truly matter for your lifestyle and well-being. If you can't quite afford everything, it's easier to let go of some desired wants when you're able to state clearly which things are essential.

Common House-Hunting Needs

- The size of living spaces, including bedrooms, bathrooms, and a functional kitchen that are essential for comfortable living.
- Closeness or further distance to work, schools, essential amenities, and transportation options can significantly impact your daily life and convenience.

- A well-maintained home with a sound foundation, sturdy walls, and a leak-free roof provides a safe and secure living environment.

Common House-Hunting Wants

- The overall style and curb appeal of a home can influence your emotional connection and personal preferences.
- Amenities like a pool, fireplace, or home office can enhance your lifestyle and provide additional enjoyment.
- A safe, friendly, and well-maintained neighborhood contributes to your overall quality of life and sense of belonging.

The Importance of Differentiating Needs From Wants

Prioritizing needs ensures you do not compromise on essential aspects that impact your daily life and well-being. By identifying your true needs, you can narrow down your search to homes that meet the fundamentals without getting swayed by every desirable feature that comes along. Moreover, it automatically eliminates houses that do not fit your needs and prevents you from emotional buying. You will barely regret your purchase if you buy a home that meets your needs more than your wants, because wants can change from time to time and can also be added on in the future.

How to Create Your Needs vs. Wants List

To make a sensible list, you must begin by identifying the essential features you cannot live without, such as the number of bedrooms and bathrooms, the location, and the overall condition of the home. Refine your list by considering additional factors that matter to you, such as natural light, storage space, or specific amenities.

LOCATION AND NEIGHBORHOOD FACTORS TO CONSIDER

When deciding where to live, the ideal location and neighborhood are specific to your individual needs, preferences, and lifestyle. Take your time, conduct thorough research, and prioritize the factors that matter most to you and your family. Choosing the right location and neighborhood for your new home is a crucial decision that can significantly impact your quality of life, commute times, and overall happiness.

Budget

Your housing budget is the primary item that will determine the neighborhoods you can afford. Determine your maximum purchase price based on your financial situation, including your mortgage preapproval amount, down payment, and potential closing costs.

The Cost of Living

Evaluate the cost of living in different areas. Consider factors like groceries, utilities, transportation, and entertainment expenses to assess whether or not that neighborhood you're interested in is really affordable. I know people who choose to live in the trendy and expensive areas of their city and while they may be able to afford the mortgage payment, that isn't the only cost. Generally, gasoline, parking costs, and food costs are higher in these areas.

Opportunities

If your job is an important factor, consider the distance to your current or potential workplace. Evaluate the local job market and career opportunities in the area to ensure your professional goals align with the location.

Amenities

If you enjoy outdoor activities, have you chosen a house that is close to parks, trails, recreational facilities, and are natural areas easily accessible? Evaluate whether the neighborhood offers outdoor pursuits that align with your lifestyle.

Neighborhood Safety

Research crime rates in different neighborhoods to make sure you choose a safe and secure environment for yourself and your family. Compare crime statistics and consider the presence of community policing initiatives.

Indicators of a Potentially Unsafe Neighborhood

- Frequent occurrences of criminal activities, such as theft, burglary, assault, or drug-related offenses, suggest a neighborhood with elevated safety concerns.
- A noticeable and consistent presence of police patrols or law enforcement vehicles may indicate ongoing criminal activity or a neighborhood struggling with crime.
- A high number of vacant, neglected, or boarded-up buildings can signal a lack of investment in the area and potentially contribute to a sense of insecurity and vulnerability.
- Littered food waste or discarded food items in public spaces can reflect a disregard for community upkeep and may attract pests or contribute to a sense of neglect.
- While not inherently a negative factor, a neighborhood with a high proportion of rental properties may indicate a transient population or a lack of long-term investment in the community.

Signs of a Safe and Vibrant Neighborhood

- Regular community gatherings, festivals, or neighborhood-wide events suggest a sense of unity and involvement among residents, fostering a positive and supportive atmosphere.
- A neighborhood with a variety of thriving local businesses, such as shops, restaurants, and cafés, indicates economic vitality and a sense of community pride.

- Children playing freely in parks, streets, or front yards is a heartwarming sign of a safe and family-friendly environment.
- A consistently low crime rate suggests a neighborhood with effective crime prevention measures and a strong sense of community vigilance.
- Well-lit streets, parks, and common areas contribute to a sense of safety and discourage criminal activity.
- Making friends with neighbors can provide valuable insights into the neighborhood's dynamics and potential safety concerns.
- A positive and responsive relationship with local law enforcement can enhance a sense of security and trust within the community.
- Active neighborhood watch programs demonstrate a proactive approach to crime prevention and foster a sense of community responsibility.

Transport Network

Evaluate the availability and efficiency of public transportation in the area, especially if you rely on it for commuting or accessing essential services. Consider the distance to public transportation stops and the overall quality of the transportation system.

Proximity to Friends and Family

Consider the distance to your friends and family when choosing a location. If you value close relationships and frequent visits, prioritize neighborhoods that are within a reasonable distance from your loved ones.

Climate Conditions

Consider the climate and weather patterns of the area. If you have specific preferences for warm or cold weather, coastal or inland locations, or the avoidance of extreme weather conditions, factor these into your decision.

Big City vs. Small Towns

Decide whether you prefer the vibrant energy and amenities of a big city or the tranquility and slower pace of a small town. Consider your lifestyle preferences, commuting tolerance, and access to services and attractions when making this choice.

Your Future Needs

Anticipate your future needs and whether the neighborhood can accommodate potential changes in your lifestyle, such as a growing family, career changes, or retirement plans. Consider the availability of schools, senior living options, and future development plans.

Knowing what you want in a home will help you stick to your goals, even in the face of challenges. It's best to follow your desires and get the basic must-have features that your home cannot do without. Once you've sorted these out, you can work on refining the property and adjusting flexible features until you achieve your dream home.

Action Steps

❑ Make a Priority List of what you must have in your new home, like the number of rooms and basic features.

❑ Separate your needs (essential things) from your wants (nice-to-have extras).

❑ Consider location and neighborhood as you think about where you want to live, based on your budget, job, safety, and amenities.

❑ Check transportation options and the local climate.

❑ Do you prefer a big city or a small town? What amenities do each have?

❑ Determine how much space you need in terms of square footage and rooms. Also consider the layout of your living areas, garage, and any extra space you might need.

❑ What's your preferred home style? Decide if you want a new or older home, considering your personal style and maintenance preferences.

Next we look at how your desires and choices will help you focus on the actual house-hunting process.

7

THE HOUSE HUNT BEGINS

House hunting is one of the most adventurous processes. It is filled with highs and lows, depending on your approach. For most homeowners, using the internet or starting the journey by themselves is where the journey began. While this may give you a sense of control, searching over numerous listings and having to refine your filters can be a more draining exercise than the actual home search. Fortunately, the majority of homebuyers also sing the praises of their real estate agents, raving about how stress-free and rewarding their home search was. And remember, it's the seller who pays the real estate fees, so why not make use of a professional's knowledge, their resources and their contacts? This chapter paints the world of house hunting and gives invaluable information on working with real estate agents to secure a perfect gem.

FINDING PROPERTIES

Finding the right property can be a daunting task, but with a bit of planning and research, you can make the process more manageable and enjoyable. Before starting on your home search, take some time to define your must-haves and nice-to-haves. It is also worth noting that finding the right property takes time, patience, and persistence. Therefore, don't get discouraged if you don't find your perfect match immediately. Keep exploring, refining your criteria, and working with your agent to stay informed about new listings.

How to Find Your Property

Utilize Real Estate Websites

Numerous online real estate platforms, such as Zillow, Trulia, and Realtor.com, provide comprehensive listings of properties available for sale or rent. These websites allow you to filter your search based on specific criteria, such as location, price range, property type, and number of bedrooms and bathrooms. You can also view property photos, virtual tours, and detailed descriptions to get a better sense of each property.

Engage Real Estate Agents

Real estate agents can be invaluable resources in your property search. They possess extensive knowledge of the local market, can provide insights into pricing trends, and can help you navigate the complexities of the buying or renting process. Reputable agents will listen to your needs, understand your preferences, and actively seek out properties that match your criteria.

Explore Newspaper Listings

While online listings have become the primary source of property information, traditional newspaper listings still offer a valuable resource. Local newspapers often feature listings for sale-by-owner properties, which may not appear on online platforms. Additionally, newspaper listings may provide more detailed descriptions and contact information for the seller or their agent.

Network With Friends, Family, and Colleagues

Let your network know you are in the market for a property. Friends, family, and colleagues may have personal connections in the real estate industry or may be aware of properties that are not yet publicly listed. Word-of-mouth can be a powerful tool in uncovering hidden gems and gaining access to off-market opportunities.

Drive Through Potential Neighborhoods

You might want to drive around the neighborhood of your interest in search of "for sale" signs. It is a good opportunity to see the amenities you like and assess the community on a surface level.

VISITING OPEN HOUSES AND SHOWINGS

Visiting open houses and showings is an essential part of the property search process. It allows you to physically inspect potential homes, assess their condition, and get a feel for the neighborhood.

How to Find Open Houses

Real Estate Websites

Check real estate websites like Zillow, Trulia, and Realtor.com for listings of open houses in your desired area. These websites allow you to filter your search based on specific criteria, such as location, price range, and property type.

Real Estate Agents

Work with a real estate agent who can provide you with a list of upcoming open houses that match your criteria. Agents often have access to off-market properties and can schedule private showings for you.

Local Newspapers

Check local newspapers for listings of open houses. While not as comprehensive as online listings, newspapers may feature properties not yet listed on major platforms.

Signs and Flyers

Be on the lookout for open house signs and flyers in the neighborhoods you're interested in. These direct advertisements can lead you to properties that may not be listed online.

Neighborhood Inquiry

Ask neighbors, local businesses, and community groups if they are aware of any upcoming open houses. Word-of-mouth can uncover hidden gems and off-market opportunities.

Benefits of Open Houses

Physical Inspection

Open houses allow you to walk through the property, assess its condition, and get a sense of its layout and space.

Visualization

You can visualize yourself living on the property, imagine your furniture arrangement, and consider how your lifestyle would fit within the space.

Neighborhood Assessment

You can observe the surrounding neighborhood, get a feel for its atmosphere, and assess its proximity to amenities and essential services.

Community Interaction

You can interact with neighbors, real estate agents, and potential buyers, gaining valuable insights and perspectives on the property and the area.

Are Your Eyes Wide Open?

Interior Features

Take a good look at the general condition of the property, watching for signs of wear, tear, or potential repairs. Consider the layout of the property. Does it meets your needs and preferences for living spaces, traffic flow, and storage? Think about the natural light in each room. You want it to provide adequate illumination and it should be a welcoming atmosphere. The quality of finishes, fixtures, and appliances will help you to decide if you need to plan for potential upgrades or renovations that may be needed. You may also want to check for adequate storage space in closets, cabinets, and other areas to store all your belongings.

Exterior Features

Stand back and look at the curb appeal of the property, taking in the landscaping, exterior maintenance, and overall look and condition of the property. Inspect the exterior for signs of structural issues, such as cracks, uneven surfaces, or foundation problems. You will want to be satisfied with the usability and appeal of outdoor spaces, such as patios, decks, or fenced-in yards. Consider the level of privacy and potential noise levels from surrounding areas or traffic. Evaluate the closeness to amenities, such as schools, parks, transportation, and shopping centers.

Upgrades

Check for energy-efficient features, such as updated windows, insulation, and appliances, to save on utility costs. Inquire about smart home features, such as automated lighting, security systems, and thermostats, for added convenience and control, if they are things you are interested in. Look for sustainable features, such as solar panels, water conservation measures, and eco-friendly materials, for environmental benefits and potential cost savings. You can also check your ability to do these upgrades yourself, as the homes that come with them are usually costly.

Red Flags to Avoid

High Inventory in the Same Neighborhood

An large number of similar properties for sale in the same area could mean there are underlying issues with the neighborhood or market conditions.

Lots of Recent Renovations

While renovations can enhance a property, excessive or poorly done renovations may be an attempt to mask underlying problems or conceal flaws.

Lots of Fragrance

An overpowering scent or excessive use of air fresheners could be used to cover up unpleasant odors or mask underlying issues.

Signs of Neglect

Visible signs of neglect, such as unkempt landscaping, overflowing gutters, or peeling paint, may indicate a lack of proper maintenance or care.

Unfinished Construction

Unless you are into undervalued, distressed properties, you'll want to avoid properties with significant unfinished construction, as it could lead to delays, cost overruns, and potential safety hazards.

HOME INSPECTIONS

A home inspection is a visual examination of a residential property, conducted by a qualified inspector, to evaluate its condition and identify any potential problems or hazards, even those that could come up in the future. The purpose of a home inspection is to provide buyers with an objective assessment of the property's current state, which will allow them to make informed decisions about their purchase. Because it's for the buyer's benefit, it's usually the buyer's responsibility to request and pay for a professional home inspection prior to finalizing the purchase to ensure that their investment is secure.

The cost of a home inspection varies depending on the size and complexity of the property, as well as the experience and credentials of the inspector. However, the average cost of a home inspection in the United States is between $275 and $400, depending on your state, square footage, or the home inspector. In some cases, a special home inspection is conducted for additional inspections such as a termite inspection or radon testing, which cost more (Kilroy, 2023).

Think you have enough experience to judge the hidden condition of a property by what you see when you tour the house? There are items and issues a qualified inspector can identify that will surprise you. This isn't a bad thing, as the more you know about a property, the better prepared you will be to make a good decision. Remember that not every identified issue is a deal-breaker, sometimes it's just the thing you need to negotiate a better deal, especially if the repair of the issue is something that can't be handled without great time or expense.

Home Inspection vs. Home Appraisal

A home inspection typically assesses the physical condition of a home, while a home appraisal deals with its market value. While both processes examine the exterior and interior of the home and essentially protect the buyer's investment, their purposes are different. An inspection is optional, while an appraisal is usually mandatory. Both the home inspection and the appraisal are paid for by the buyer, except in the case of some government-backed loans where the seller must make repairs, in which case, the lender may cover the costs of a home appraisal. In most transactions, whether or not the seller will repair issues uncovered by the inspection is part of the negotiation process, except in those cases where a seller is selling "As-Is" which means they will make no repairs.

What to Expect During an Inspection

A home inspection typically takes 1–2 hours, unless there are serious issues with the house. You can expect that an inspector will find some blemishes that the seller did not mention or was not aware of. Where an inspector insists on a follow-up inspection on serious matters like termite inspection or radon testing, you can expect follow-up costs.

Red Flags for Home Inspectors

Electrical Faults

Electrical faults can cause serious safety hazards, and they are often difficult to spot without the proper training and equipment. An experienced home inspector will check for signs of outdated wiring, overloaded circuits, and faulty outlets, which you might overlook.

Foundation Cracks

Foundation cracks can indicate underlying structural problems that could compromise the integrity of your home. These cracks can be caused by settling, soil movement, or moisture damage. A home inspector will have the expertise to identify these cracks and assess their severity, something you might not be able to do on your own.

Drywall Cracks

Drywall cracks can indicate underlying structural problems or moisture damage. Home inspectors will carefully examine the walls for any signs of cracks, and if found, they will assess their severity and recommend further evaluation if necessary.

Worn-Out Roofing

A worn-out roof can lead to leaks, water damage, and mold growth. The inspector will check for signs of wear and tear, such as missing or damaged shingles, sagging rooflines, and granules in the gutters. They will also be able to assess the overall condition of the roof and provide you with an estimate of its lifespan.

Run-Down Decks

Run-down decks can pose safety hazards due to rotting or splintering wood, loose or missing nails or screws, sagging or uneven deck boards, and damaged railings. Home inspectors will thoroughly inspect the deck for these issues.

Galvanized Pipes

Galvanized pipes were commonly used in older homes, but they are prone to corrosion and rust, which can lead to leaks and water damage. A professional inspector will be able to identify galvanized pipes and assess their condition. They can also provide you with recommendations on replacing them with copper or PEX pipes to avoid future problems.

Grading and Drainage Issues

Proper grading and drainage are essential for preventing water from pooling around a home's foundation. If the ground slopes toward the house or there are drainage ditches that are not functioning properly, it can lead to water damage, mold growth, and foundation problems. An experienced home inspector will be able to assess the grading and drainage around your potential home and identify any potential issues.

Sewer Issues

Sewer problems can be messy, unpleasant, and expensive to fix. Signs of sewer issues include slow drains, gurgling sounds from pipes, and sewage back-ups. Proper inspection will reveal signs of sewer problems and recommend further inspection or repair if necessary.

Mold

Mold can cause respiratory problems and other health issues, so it is important to identify and address mold growth in your home. Home inspections will unearth signs of mold, such as musty odors, visible mold growth, and water damage. They will also be able to assess the extent of the mold infestation and provide recommendations for remediation.

HVAC Havoc

A properly functioning HVAC system is essential for maintaining a comfortable indoor temperature. An experienced home inspector will check the condition of the HVAC system, including the furnace, air conditioner, and ductwork. They will be able to identify any problems with the system and provide you with an estimate of the cost of repairs or replacement.

FINDING THE RIGHT REAL ESTATE AGENT

Navigating the complex world of real estate can be a daunting task, especially for first-time buyers or sellers. One of the most critical decisions you will make in this process is choosing the right real estate agent. A skilled and experienced agent can guide you through the intricacies of the market, advocate for your best interests, and help you achieve your real estate goals.

Real Estate Agent Basics

Buyer's Agent

A buyer's agent represents you, the buyer, in purchasing a property. They work exclusively for you, making sure your interests are prioritized throughout the transaction. Buyer's agents typically have deep knowledge of the local market, can help you find suitable properties, and guide you through the negotiation and closing process.

Listing Agent

A listing agent represents the seller in marketing and selling their property. They are responsible for creating an enticing listing, attracting potential buyers, and negotiating the sale on the seller's behalf. Listing agents have extensive experience in pricing properties competitively and maximizing the seller's return on investment.

Realtor vs. Real Estate Agent

The terms "realtor" and "real estate agent" are often used interchangeably, but there is a subtle distinction. A realtor is a licensed member of the NAR. To become a realtor, individuals must adhere to a strict code of ethics and undergo additional training compared to nonrealtor agents. A real estate agent is licensed in the state they work in, and they abide by state and national laws.

Real Estate Agent vs. Broker

A real estate agent is a licensed professional who assists buyers, sellers, or both in real estate transactions. They can work independently but in most states must work under a real estate broker. A real estate broker, on the other hand, has a higher level of licensure that allows them to manage and supervise other real estate agents. Brokers typically have more experience and can provide a wider range of services.

Why Should You Use a Real Estate Agent?

Searching for Your Home Is an Agent's Priority

Real estate agents are experts in the market, spending their days understanding trends, researching properties, and navigating the complexities of buying and selling homes. They have the knowledge and experience to guide you through the process efficiently and effectively. Even if you can spare a few minutes to create home search alerts on multiple listing platforms, you cannot give them as much attention as an agent would. Remember, it is their day job, so that is what they do best and will prioritize until they find the house you want.

They Keep a Look Out for Potential House Problems

Beyond the cosmetic appeal, real estate agents can identify underlying issues with a property that may not be apparent to an untrained eye. They can assess structural integrity, potential renovation needs, and potential code violations, saving you from costly surprises down the road. They can see a home's real problems that you may overlook.

They Can Help You See Your Home's Investment Potential

In most cases, your main focus when looking for a home is imagining yourself living there, not particularly making any money from it. However, real estate agents can help you identify properties with strong investment potential, weighing factors like location, neighborhood trends, and potential for value appreciation. They can guide you in making informed decisions in keeping with your long-term financial goals. Real estate agents can also help you understand what needs to be done to increase the value of the property before you buy it. They can suggest renovations, improvements, or staging techniques that can enhance the property's appeal and maximize its resale value.

Avoid Code Violations

Without an experienced real estate agent, you could risk buying a house with hidden code violations that could lead to expensive repairs or legal issues. Agents can spot potential code violations and advise you on the necessary steps to address them.

Your Personal Tour Guide

Real estate agents act as your personal tour guides through the city. They know the local routes and logistics of the area and are in a better position to guide you on how to move around and go from place to place.

Who You Know Matters More Than What You Know

The real estate market is often driven by personal connections. Agents have established relationships with other agents, lenders, contractors, and industry professionals, which can give you an advantage in finding the right property, securing favorable financing, or negotiating the best terms. Most real estate agents also have personal connections to local contractors, ensuring you have access to reputable and reliable professionals for renovations, repairs, or maintenance work. They can help you compare estimates, negotiate pricing, and oversee the work to ensure it meets your standards.

Protect Your Interests in Negotiations

Real estate transactions involve complex negotiations, and an experienced agent will be your advocate, fighting for your best interests. They can strategize, negotiate on your behalf, and ensure the final agreement aligns with your financial goals and expectations.

Digital Resources Do Not Address the Emotional Side

While online resources and listing platforms provide valuable information, they cannot replace the human touch and emotional intelligence of a real estate agent. Agents can help you navigate the emotional roller-coaster of buying or selling a home, providing support, guidance, and reassurance throughout the process.

Home Inspection Findings

Upon receiving a list of home inspection findings, you may not be sure what to ask for in terms of repairs or concessions. An experienced agent can help you interpret the findings, prioritize the necessary repairs, and negotiate appropriate remedies with the seller.

Transaction Paperwork

Real estate transactions involve a mountain of paperwork, from contracts and disclosures to financing documents and title transfers. An agent will handle the tedious paperwork, ensuring all documents are accurately completed, filed, and processed on time.

Where to Find Real Estate Agents

Your Personal Network

Ask friends, family members, or colleagues who have recently bought or sold a home for recommendations. They can provide firsthand insights into the agent's work ethic, communication style, and overall performance. Additionally, seek referrals from professionals you trust, such as your financial advisor, mortgage lender, or property manager. These individuals may have worked with reputable agents and can provide valuable recommendations based on your specific needs. Moreover, check with neighbors, local businesses, or community groups for recommendations. They may have valuable insights into agents who have experience in your area and understand the local market dynamics.

Research

Utilize real estate websites like Zillow, Trulia, or Realtor.com to search for agents in your area. These websites allow you to filter your search based on criteria like experience, designations, and client reviews. Social media platforms like Facebook, LinkedIn, or Nextdoor can be an invaluable way to connect with local agents and read reviews from past clients. Engage with their online presence to assess their personality, communication style, and engagement with the community. You can also check online review sites like Yelp, Google Reviews, or RateMyAgent to read feedback from past clients. Pay attention to patterns in reviews to gauge the agent's strengths, weaknesses, and overall client satisfaction.

Official Referral Sources

Contact your local or state real estate association for a list of recommended agents. These associations often maintain a database of reputable agents who adhere to ethical standards and have a proven track record. Additionally, you can access multiple listing services (MLSs) through a real estate agent or an online platform. MLS listings often include the contact information of the listing agent, allowing you to reach out directly for more information. Visit local real estate brokerages to inquire about their agents. Brokerages can provide information about their agents' experience, areas of expertise, and availability to take on new clients.

Contact Referral Agents

If you are relocating to a new area, consider working with a referral agent. Referral agents specialize in connecting clients with reputable agents in their desired location, using their network and relationships to facilitate a smooth transition. If you are working with a relocation company, they may have a network of preferred real estate agents in your destination city. Also, if your employer has a relocation services program, they may provide you with a list of recommended agents in your new location. These agents can be helpful in navigating an unfamiliar market and prioritizing your relocation needs.

Choosing the Right Real Estate Agent

Experience

Choose an agent with a proven track record in the type of property you are interested in, which in this case is a residential home.

Relevant Certifications

Ensure the agent holds a valid real estate license from the state where you intend to buy or sell. You may also want to look for an agent who is a member of the NAR. NAR membership indicates adherence to a strict code of ethics and ongoing education. It is also crucial to check if the agent holds any specialized designations, such as Certified Residential Specialist (CRS), Certified Luxury Home Marketing Specialist (CLHMS), or Senior Real Estate Specialist (SRES). These designations demonstrate expertise in specific areas of the market.

Marketing and Technical Skills

The real estate agent's marketing and technical skills will matter when you are selling your property. Assess the agent's marketing skills, especially if you're selling. You must inquire about their strategies for attracting buyers, showcasing your property, and utilizing online and offline marketing channels effectively. Verify the agent's proficiency in using real estate technology, such as listing platforms, property management tools, and online marketing tools. Technological competence can enhance their efficiency and effectiveness.

Communication Skills

Evaluate the agent's communication and interpersonal skills. Ensure they can clearly explain market trends, complex real estate processes, and financial information in a way you understand.

Knowledge of the Local Market

Seek out an agent who has extensive knowledge of the specific neighborhoods or areas you are considering. Their familiarity with local market trends, amenities, and potential drawbacks can be invaluable.

Availability

Consider the agent's availability to meet your needs and schedule. Discuss their response time to inquiries, willingness to work with the times you are available, and their ability to be present during key stages of the process.

Level of Personal Attention

Choose an agent whose personality and working style align with yours. Find someone who listens attentively, understands your goals, and can navigate negotiations effectively on your behalf.

Commitment and Contracts

You want the agent's level of commitment to the transaction to be focused on your needs and wants as you start your house hunt. Inquire about their experience in similar situations, their dedication to representing your best interests, and their ability to handle challenging negotiations effectively. In the real estate world, things will not always work out as planned, so you must carefully review any contracts or agreements you sign with the agent. Understand the terms of their commission structure, the agent's responsibilities, and the termination clause in case your needs change, or you are dissatisfied with their services.

How to Interview Real Estate Agents

Interviewing potential real estate agents is a crucial step in finding the right partner for your homebuying or selling journey. It is essential to interview multiple agents to compare their experience, expertise, and personalities. Below are some key questions to ask during your interviews.

Experience and Expertise

- How long have you been a real estate agent?
- What is your area of expertise? (residential, commercial, investment properties, etc.)
- How many homes have you sold or helped buyers find in the past year?
- What are your designations or specialized training in real estate?

Market Knowledge and Local Insights

- How well do you know the neighborhoods in my desired area?
- What are the current market trends and pricing patterns in this area?
- What are the potential challenges or opportunities for buyers or sellers in this market?
- Can you provide insights into local amenities, schools, and community resources?

Communication and Availability

- How will you communicate with me throughout the process?
- How quickly do you typically respond to inquiries and emails?
- What is your availability for scheduling appointments and showings?
- How do you handle conflicts or unexpected issues that arise during a transaction?

Marketing and Negotiation Strategies

- How will you market my property if I am selling?
- What tools and strategies do you use to attract potential buyers?
- How do you approach negotiations to achieve the best outcome for your clients?
- What is your average sales-to-list ratio?

Fees and Commission Structure

- What is your commission structure for buyers and sellers?
- What additional fees or costs should I be aware of?
- How do you handle multiple offers or bidding wars?
- What is your policy on commission reimbursement or refunds if the transaction falls through?

Personal Connection and Referrals

- Why should I choose you as my real estate agent?
- Can you provide me with references from past clients?
- What is your approach to building long-term relationships with your clients?
- How do you stay up-to-date with industry changes and legal regulations?

CONSIDER YOUR FUTURE NEEDS

When buying your home, you may want to have an exit strategy. What do you plan to do with the house in the future? Some buyers prefer to stay in their homes for as long as it benefits them and their families and later retire to a smaller and more affordable home. Others may choose to sell the house and reinvest the money in another viable property or rent it out. Another common exit strategy many homeowners use is to access their equity and use it to finance their other financial dreams instead of selling the house to get cash for those dreams.

Equity Release or HELOC

There is more than one type of equity release which is the ability to access the value of your home equity—the portion that you own versus the share owned by the mortgage company—and turn it into tax-free cash you can use for other personal goals. There are things to consider before releasing your equity, such as the current market value of the property and your inheritance options. These loan types are typically accessible to homeowners aged 55 and above, as they are likely to have paid off or nearly paid off their mortgage. Using the money from your equity means your descendants will get less inheritance upon your death. With the help of a financial advisor, you can release your equity using any of the options below.

Lifetime or Reverse Mortgage

With a lifetime or reverse mortgage, you take out a loan against the equity in your home. The loan has no monthly payments and does not need to be repaid until you die or move into long-term care. You can choose to receive the money as a lump sum or as regular payments, depending upon how much equity you need out at the time you get the loan. Think of it like a backwards payment, instead of paying a monthly mortgage payment, all the loan payments and interest you would have paid over the life of loan are added up and due when the borrower dies. This affects the estate and what will be left to your descendants, so you need to think carefully about this type of loan. The biggest benefit is to the retired as they continue into their elderly years as this type loan allows them to have cash while they stay in their home.

Home Reversion Plans

With a home reversion plan, you sell part or all of your home to a home reversion company in exchange for a lump sum or regular payments. You will continue to live in the home until you die or move into long-term care. You run the risk that if inflation drives home prices up during the time of this type loan you have signed away all your rights to that increase in value. The main difference between this type loan and a lifetime or reverse mortgage is that you've already sold the property so once you die, there are no possible assets to leave to your descendants.

The main idea of this chapter was to help you find the property that meets your needs, as you identified them in the previous chapter. Working with professional real estate agents will make it easier for you to find what you would like to have in a home.

Action Steps

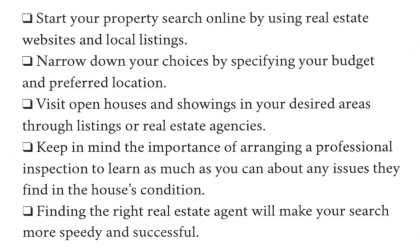

❑ Start your property search online by using real estate websites and local listings.
❑ Narrow down your choices by specifying your budget and preferred location.
❑ Visit open houses and showings in your desired areas through listings or real estate agencies.
❑ Keep in mind the importance of arranging a professional inspection to learn as much as you can about any issues they find in the house's condition.
❑ Finding the right real estate agent will make your search more speedy and successful.

❏ Get recommendations for real estate agents from friends or family.

❏ Interview multiple agents to find one who understands your needs and is a good fit for you.

On to the step in this journey that everyone wants to know about: how to make a winning offer on that house that meets your criteria.

8

MAKING AN OFFER

Getting the property you want is not as simple as just offering the property's purchase price in full. Nor is it as easy as offering a low ball offer with the assumption you'll get a great deal. There is a lot more competition in some cities than in others, where getting your dream home may require fast action, strategic moves, and a motivated offer. Making your offer stand out during bidding wars takes a lot of effort. On the flip side, you want to make sure you don't overpay for a property or leave value on the bargaining table. This chapter will help structure your offer to appeal more to buyers, especially in a competitive market.

A GUIDE TO MAKING AN OFFER

Making the right offer to purchase a home depends on the market direction. If there are more houses than there are buyers, you will be in a better position to negotiate a better deal. However, you may need to motivate acceptance of your offer in a competitive seller's market. You must also be careful not to go beyond your budget during bid wars. It's easy to strain your budget when competition is high and you get caught up in offering more to get the house you want. You might win the bid, but if you can't afford what you offer, then you haven't won even if you end up with the property.

Step 1: Review Comparable Listings

Before making an offer on a house, it is essential to understand the current market value of similar properties in the area. This will help you come up with a fair and competitive price to offer. A real estate agent can provide you with comparable listings and help you analyze the features and amenities of each property to make an informed decision.

Step 2: Be Strategic With Timing Your Offer

The timing of your offer can significantly impact whether or not it is accepted. If you submit an offer too early in the listing process, you may be competing with fewer buyers, but you also may not have a clear understanding of the seller's true expectations. On the other hand, if you wait too long, you may face more competition and risk the property going under contract with another buyer before you have a chance to make an offer.

Step 3: Use Cash as Leverage

In a competitive market, offering cash for a property can give you a significant advantage over buyers who need to get their financing in place. Sellers often prefer cash offers because they close faster and reduce the risk of the deal falling through due to financial contingencies.

Step 4: Stand Out as a Buyer

If you are making an offer in a competitive market, you must stand out as a buyer to win bid wars. Getting a preapproval is one way to show your seriousness and readiness to close a deal. You may also have to make a higher offer; however, price is not your only bargaining chip. Find out what is important to the seller, and tailor your offer around that. You can connect with the seller and demonstrate your personal attachment to the house by sharing your vision of raising a family there or by acknowledging their effort to keep the property in good condition.

WHAT DOES THE OFFER INCLUDE?

Earnest Money

Earnest money is a deposit of funds that demonstrates your seriousness as a buyer and is held in escrow until the closing of the transaction. The amount of earnest money is typically 1%–10% of the purchase price (Chen, 2023). You can offer more if you are buying in a competitive market.

Contingencies

These are conditions that must be met before the sale can proceed. Common contingencies include obtaining financing approval, satisfactory home inspection results, and a clear title to the property.

Property Description

The offer should clearly identify the property being purchased and provide a detailed description of its features and amenities. It must also include the address and exact house number.

Clear Title

The offer should state that the buyer expects to receive a clear title to the property, free of any liens or encumbrances. This means that the seller must ensure that they fully own the property and that there are no disputes or possible wars over it.

Purchase Price

The offer should clearly state the price you are willing to pay for the property.

Closing Cost Details

The offer must also include a clear and elaborate list of closing costs and who will cover them. These include loan origination fees, escrow fees, title insurance, recording fees, appraisal fees, and taxes. In a less competitive market, some sellers cover the closing costs for the buyer; however, closing costs are typically the buyer's responsibility.

Closing Date

The offer should specify the date on which you expect the sale to be finalized and the property to be transferred to your ownership.

Offer Expiration Date

An offer to purchase a home typically includes an expiration date, which is the deadline for the seller to accept or reject the offer. The expiration date is typically a few days after the offer is submitted, but it can be negotiated between the buyer and seller.

Signatures

Both the buyer and the seller, along with their authorized representatives, must sign the offer. An unsigned offer is not official.

Other Provisions

In addition to the basic terms of the purchase price, earnest money deposit, and closing date, an offer to purchase a home may also include various other provisions. These provisions can range from contingencies that protect the buyer's interests to specific requests regarding the condition of the property. Generally it is understood that any features of the house that are permanently attached will remain with the house, but it is good practice to list any items that it looks like the seller added and might want to take with them. That's if you want them to stay. You may be thrilled about that wall to ceiling bookcase they have in the bonus room, or you may want to make sure they detach it and take it with them.

FACTORS TO CONSIDER WHEN MAKING AN OFFER

It is crucial to consider various factors to ensure you make an informed and competitive offer. While you must be ready to spend more money to outbid other buyers, it is important to analyze the type of market and remember your financial goals.

Your Budget

Your budget is the primary factor that determines the price range you can afford. Consider your preapproved mortgage amount, down payment, and potential closing costs to establish a realistic budget.

Type of Market

Understand the current market conditions, whether it is a buyer's or seller's market. In a buyer's market, you may have more negotiating power, while in a seller's market, you may need to be more flexible and willing to offer a higher price.

Comparative Market Analysis

A comparative market analysis provides insights into comparable properties that have recently sold in the area. This analysis helps you determine a fair market value and understand the pricing trends for similar homes.

Neighborhood Market Data

Research the specific neighborhood where the property is located. What are the crime rates, school quality, amenities, and overall desirability of the property? Will these add to or detract from the value and potential appreciation of the home? Answers to these questions with help guide your decision.

Financial Profile

Your financial profile, including your credit score, DTI ratio, and employment history, influence your ability to get the loan that will work best for you. A strong financial profile makes you a more attractive buyer to the seller.

Physical Condition of the Home

Obtain a comprehensive home inspection to determine the condition of the property. Identify any structural issues, repairs needed, or potential renovations required and factor them into your offer.

Seller Motivation

Understanding the seller's motivation can influence your negotiation strategy. If the seller is motivated to sell quickly, you may have more leverage to negotiate a lower price or favorable terms.

Days on Market

The number of days a property has been on the market indicates the level of buyer interest and the seller's willingness to negotiate.

162 | V J DEAN

A larger days-on-market (DOM) figure may signal a property that is overpriced or has issues, while a shorter DOM suggests increased competition and a need to submit a strong offer.

Your Desire for the Home

Consider your emotional attachment to the property. While it's important to make a rational decision based on market conditions and your financial situation, do not let your desire for the home cloud your judgment.

COMMON TYPES OF HOMEBUYING CONTINGENCIES

Home Inspection Contingency

Home inspection contingencies allow the buyer to have the property inspected by a qualified professional to identify any structural, mechanical, or other issues. If the inspection reveals significant defects that are not acceptable to the buyer, the contract can be canceled without penalty.

Appraisal Contingency

An appraisal contingency guarantees that the contract will go forward if the property is appraised for a value that is the same or higher than the agreed-upon purchase price. If the appraisal comes in lower than the offer price, the buyer may have the option to negotiate with the seller for a lower price or cancel the contract. If the buyer still wants to go ahead, he can pay cash for the portion of the value of the property above the appraisal amount. This is a risky strategy that you would only want to do if you as buyer were sure that the value of the property will continue to rise.

Financing Contingency

Financing contingencies give the buyer time to finalize the financing for the purchase of the property. If the buyer is unable to obtain a mortgage or other financing within the specified time-frame, they can cancel the contract and receive their earnest money back.

Home Sale Contingency

A home sale contingency is typically used by buyers who are selling their current home before purchasing a new one. It allows the buyer to make an offer on the new property without having to worry about carrying two mortgages simultaneously. If the buyer's current home doesn't sell within a specified period, they can cancel the contract on the new property.

Importance of Contingencies

Contingencies are essential for protecting buyers in real estate transactions. They provide a safety net and allow buyers to back out of the deal if they discover unforeseen issues with the property or are unable to secure financing.

Preventing Contingencies From Hindering the Process

While contingencies are crucial, it's important to manage them effectively to avoid delays or complications in the closing process. It must be clear that the seller understands the contingencies and the potential impact on the transaction. Establish clear timelines for completing inspections, obtaining appraisals, and securing financing. If any issues arise during the contingency period, work together with the seller to find solutions and keep the transaction moving forward. In a competitive market, waiving contingencies can make your offer more attractive to sellers. However, it's important to carefully weigh the risks and benefits before doing so.

The offer you make on a house depends on the market. You may either have to act fast, motivate your offer with a sizable amount of earnest money, or prove that you are a serious buyer in a competitive market. In the buyer's market, you have the upper hand to negotiate better terms.

NEGOTIATE CLOSING COSTS

Closing costs typically range from 2%–5% of the purchase price. You can negotiate closing costs with the seller to try to reduce your overall cost of purchasing the home. This may involve asking the seller to pay for certain fees or splitting the costs evenly.

COMPLETE THE HOME INSPECTION

A home inspection is a professional evaluation of the condition of a property. It is important to have a home inspection completed before finalizing the purchase of a home to identify any potential defects or problems with the property.

GET A PEST INSPECTION

A pest inspection is a professional inspection of a property to identify any signs of pests, such as termites, cockroaches, or rodents. Pest infestations can cause significant damage to a property and can be costly to repair. If the pest inspection reveals any pest infestation, buyers may negotiate with the seller to have the infestation treated or to lower the purchase price.

RENEGOTIATE THE OFFER

After the home inspection and pest inspection, you may need to renegotiate the offer with the seller. This may involve asking the seller to make repairs, lower the purchase price, or provide other concessions. Renegotiations should be done in a spirit of cooperation and compromise. The goal is to reach an agreement that is fair to both the buyer and the seller.

REMOVE CONTINGENCIES

If all contingencies are met, the purchase of the home can proceed. However, if any of the contingencies are not met, you can cancel the contract and receive your earnest money back.

Action Steps

❑ Check comparable listings by looking at similar homes that recently sold in the area to decide on a fair offer price.
❑ Time your offer wisely by understanding the market's condition and submitting your offer at the right time to increase your chances of acceptance.
❑ Offering cash can make your offer attractive to the seller.

Work with your real estate agent for ideas on other ways to put your offer in first place, such as terms that will show the seller to your interest and flexibility, and be open to adjusting those terms to meet their needs.

❏ Once the offer is an accepted contract, it's the time to focus on dealing with any contingencies to keep the contract headed to the finish line.

With contingencies handled, the next step is moving through the closing process, which is detailed in the next chapter.

NAVIGATING THE CLOSING PROCESS

R esearch indicates that most people go through buyer's remorse over their home purchase after reaching the closing phase. Imagine going through this lengthy process, fully committed to learning the tricks of the trade, and after all the negotiations, only to not be happy in the end. This is the time to be looking forward to moving into your new home and enjoying your new life there, not regretting such a phenomenal moment. Making good decisions at each step will help you to be content when you get to the end of the process; you have finally secured the home of your dreams. This chapter signifies that the hard work is over; however, you still need to understand the closing process and all that it includes.

A GUIDE TO REAL ESTATE CLOSING

Closing a home sale is a significant milestone in the homebuying process. It means ownership is now in your name and it's the completion of months or even years of searching and negotiation.

While the process may seem daunting, it is typically streamlined and involves a series of well-defined steps to ensure a smooth transition.

Preclosing Activities

Before the official closing date, there are several crucial steps to complete.

Loan Approval

Obtain final approval for your mortgage loan from your chosen lender. This process means your loan application has gone to underwriting and this step will involve providing the necessary documentation and verifying your financial standing so that the lender can approve your loan.

Lock in Your Interest Rate

Interest rates can fluctuate significantly, so it is important for buyers to lock in their interest rate as soon as possible. This will help to protect you from rising interest rates and keep your monthly mortgage payments predictable. You can lock in your interest rate by obtaining a mortgage commitment from a lender. This commitment will guarantee the interest rate for a certain period, typically 30–60 days.

Meet Funding Requirements

In order to finalize the purchase of a home, you must be prepared to bring your share of cash that is required for your mortgage.

This typically involves providing documentation of your income, assets, and debts to the lender.

Title Search and Insurance

A title search is completed to ensure there are no liens or encumbrances on the property's title. Title insurance protects the buyer from any potential title defects that may arise in the future.

Homeowners Insurance

Purchase homeowner's insurance to protect your investment from potential damage or loss. Your lender will not fund the loan without this protection.

Finalize Closing Costs

Work with your real estate agent and lender to calculate and finalize the closing costs, which may include appraisal fees, title insurance premiums, and escrow fees.

The Closing Meeting

The closing meeting is the formal event where the transfer of ownership occurs. It typically takes place at the escrow company's office or a designated title company.

Review and Sign Documents

Carefully review and sign all closing documents, including the purchase agreement, mortgage note, and deed of trust. A Notary Public will be present to notarize all signatures on the documents.

Provide Closing Costs

Bring certified funds, such as a cashier's check or wire transfer, to cover the closing costs. It's wise to prepare ahead on this piece, as it may take a day or more to get the funds transferred. You can't just pull out your checkbook to write a personal check, nor can you use a credit card or debit card. It doesn't matter what's in your Apple Wallet, the funds have to be verified as "cash" which means a cashier's check or wire transfer.

Sign Closing Disclosure

Review and sign the closing disclosure, which provides a summary of the transaction, including the loan terms, closing costs, and final purchase price.

UNDERSTANDING THE ROLE OF ESCROW COMPANIES

Escrow companies play a crucial role in the house-closing process, ensuring a smooth and secure transfer of funds and property ownership. They serve as neutral third parties, acting as intermediaries between buyers, sellers, and various parties involved in the transaction. Escrow fees typically cost 1%–2% of the purchase price (Dehan, 2023a). There is no rule that states who exactly must pay the escrow fees; it is up to you and the seller to agree on who will settle them.

Key Responsibilities of Escrow Companies

Collect and Hold Funds

Escrow companies collect earnest money deposits, down payments, and proceeds from the mortgage lender. They hold these funds in a secure account until the closing date.

Verify and Disburse Funds

Upon closing, escrow companies verify the validity of all financial documents and disburse funds to the appropriate parties, including the seller, mortgage lender, real estate agents, and title companies.

Prepare Closing Documents

Escrow companies prepare and handle various closing documents, including purchase agreements, deed transfers, and loan documents.

Facilitate Communication

They act as a communication hub, coordinating with buyers, sellers, lenders, and title companies to keep everyone informed throughout the process.

Ensure Title Clearance

Escrow companies work with title companies to ensure the property's title is free from liens or encumbrances, protecting the buyer's ownership rights.

Handle Disbursements and Payments

They handle the disbursement of funds to various parties involved in the closing process, ensuring all financial obligations are met.

Provide Escrow Account Statements

Escrow companies provide account statements to buyers and sellers, detailing the flow of funds and ensuring transparency throughout the process.

Handle Property Taxes and Insurance

They may assist in collecting and paying property taxes and homeowners insurance premiums, ensuring these obligations are met.

Benefits of Using an Escrow Company

Neutral Third Party

Escrow companies act as unbiased intermediaries, ensuring a fair and transparent process for all parties involved.

Secure Fund Management

They safeguard funds and ensure their proper disbursement at the appropriate time, preventing financial discrepancies.

Reduced Risk of Errors

Escrow companies handle complex financial transactions with expertise, minimizing the risk of errors or delays.

Streamlined Closing Process

They streamline the closing process by coordinating with various parties and handling the paperwork, reducing the burden on buyers and sellers.

Reduced Stress and Anxiety

By managing the financial aspects and ensuring a smooth closing, escrow companies help alleviate stress and anxiety for buyers and sellers.

THE IMPORTANCE OF HIRING AN ATTORNEY

We have already established that buying a house is one of the biggest steps you can take. It is crucial to ensure that the contract in this legal process is as secure as possible. Hiring an attorney for a house closing can be a valuable decision that provides several benefits and protections for both buyers and sellers. Most attorneys charge an hourly rate, which can be quite difficult to estimate as no one can anticipate how long the meeting will be. You can ask for a flat rate, which typically varies according to state and is estimated at $750–$1,250 for a simple house closing and $1,500–$3,000 for a more complex case (Whyte, 2023).

Legal Expertise and Guidance

Attorneys possess in-depth knowledge of real estate laws, contract terms, and legal procedures related to property transactions. They can provide guidance and explanations to help you understand the legal implications of the closing process and ensure your rights are protected.

Review and Negotiation of Documents

Attorneys can thoroughly review and analyze complex legal documents, such as purchase agreements, title documents, and mortgage terms, to identify any potential issues or discrepancies. They can also negotiate on your behalf to ensure favorable terms and protect your interests.

Title Review and Protection

Attorneys can conduct a thorough title search to identify any liens, encumbrances, or other claims on the property's title. They can also help you obtain title insurance to protect your ownership rights in case of any hidden defects or title issues.

Disclosure Compliance

Attorneys can ensure that all necessary disclosures are made accurately and in compliance with relevant laws and regulations. They can also advise you on any potential disclosures you may need to provide as a buyer or seller.

Representation and Advocacy

Attorneys act as your representatives and advocates throughout the closing process. They can communicate on your behalf, address any concerns or disputes that arise, and ensure your interests are prioritized.

Risk Mitigation and Protection

Attorneys can help identify and mitigate potential risks associated with the transaction, such as property defects, zoning issues, or potential legal claims. They can also advise you on ways to minimize liability and protect your financial interests.

Peace of Mind and Reduced Stress

By handling the legal aspects of the closing process, attorneys can alleviate stress and anxiety for buyers and sellers. They provide peace of mind by ensuring that your rights are protected and the transaction is legally sound.

TITLE COMPANIES

Title companies play a crucial role in the real estate industry, providing essential services to ensure the smooth transfer of property ownership and protect the rights of buyers and sellers. They conduct thorough title searches, issue title insurance, and handle various aspects of the closing process.

Core Responsibilities of Title Companies

Title Search and Examination

Title companies conduct a comprehensive search of public records to identify any liens, encumbrances, or other claims on the property's title. This process involves examining court records, property tax records, and other relevant documents to ensure the seller has a clear and marketable title to the property.

Title Insurance

Title companies issue title insurance policies to protect buyers and lenders from financial losses due to defects in the property's title. These policies cover a wide range of potential issues, such as hidden liens, forged deeds, and undiscovered encumbrances.

Title Closing Services

Title companies handle various aspects of the closing process, including the following:

Collecting and Disbursing Funds

They collect earnest money deposits, down payments, and proceeds from the mortgage lender and disburse these funds to the appropriate parties at closing.

Preparing Closing Documents

They prepare and finalize closing documents, such as purchase agreements, deed transfers, and loan documents, ensuring the accuracy and legal validity of these documents.

Coordinating With Parties Involved

They act as a communication hub, coordinating with buyers, sellers, lenders, and other parties involved in the transaction to ensure a smooth and timely closing.

Escrow Services

Title companies may also provide escrow services, acting as neutral third parties to hold funds and facilitate the transfer of ownership and payments between buyers, sellers, and lenders.

Benefits of Title Companies for Buyers and Sellers

Peace of Mind and Protection

Title companies provide peace of mind for both buyers and sellers by ensuring a clear title to the property and protecting against potential financial losses due to title defects.

Reduced Risk of Delays

By conducting thorough title searches and resolving title issues upfront, title companies help minimize the risk of delays or complications during the closing process.

Facilitation of Smooth Closing

Title companies streamline the closing process by handling various administrative tasks, coordinating with parties involved, and ensuring the timely transfer of funds and property ownership.

Expertise and Guidance

Title companies possess in-depth knowledge of real estate laws, title issues, and closing procedures. They can provide expert guidance to buyers and sellers throughout the transaction process.

Protection of Financial Investments

Title insurance protects the significant financial investment made by buyers and lenders in the property, safeguarding their rights and minimizing the risk of financial losses.

Compliance With Legal Requirements

Title companies ensure that all necessary legal requirements and disclosures are met throughout the transaction, protecting buyers and sellers from potential legal liabilities.

Dispute Resolution and Mediation

In the event of title-related disputes or disagreements, title companies can act as mediators and facilitate amicable resolutions to protect the interests of all parties involved.

Closing a house purchase deal is as important as when you started the process. It can be complex, hence the need to engage professionals to help you through it. Do not underestimate the closing costs, and look for opportunities to negotiate them with the seller. After this final step, you are finally ready to move into your new home. The next chapter contains tips to make the process more fun and less stressful.

Post-Closing Activities

Once the closing meeting is complete, there are a few final steps to take.

Receive Closing Documents

Obtain copies of all signed closing documents for your records.

Obtain Keys

Collect the keys to your new home from the seller or escrow agent.

Update Insurance and Utilities

Notify your insurance company about the new property and update your utility service providers.

Schedule Move-in

Plan and coordinate your move-in date, and arrange for any necessary movers or transportation.

Action Steps

❑ Prepare for closing by answering any questions or any request from the escrow or title company as they prepare the closing documents and paperwork.

❑ Your lender and his loan underwriting department will be asking questions and needing copies of your financial information. Make these requests a priority as this can make or break your goal of getting your loan in place.

❑ Items that must be in place before the closing date: home-owner's insurance; lock in your interest rate; and understand your loan terms.

❑ Be prepared to attend the schedule closing with your share of closing funds in hand - either a cashier's check or wired funds to arrive at the escrow or title company before the scheduled closing.

❑ Review all papers with an attorney or closing officer.

❑ Sign the documents and make payments. Collect your keys!

❑ After closing follow-up to make sure you receive copies of all signed documents, all closing papers and the title company insurance policy stating you have the only title to the property.

The day that seemed to take forever to come is now here - Moving Day! Plans for this day are further detailed in the next chapter.

MOVING INTO YOUR NEW HOME

Congratulations on taking the exciting leap into homeownership; despite all the effort it took to get here, you are finally in your own home! Taking this journey marks a significant milestone, and you have every reason to be proud of yourself for making it this far. As you settle into your new abode, it is natural to feel a mix of anticipation and excitement, but also some uncertainty about the process of moving in. To help ease your transition and make the most of this new chapter, let's look at some practical tips and techniques to ensure a smooth and enjoyable experience.

PREPARING AND PLANNING FOR YOUR MOVE

Most of us have moved in our lives and we know it can be a daunting task, but what's more exciting than moving into your new home! With careful planning and preparation, you can make the process smoother and less stressful. Get started on that list!

- What needs to be done in your current home before you move out?
- When do you plan to move and start packing your stuff?
- What's the distance between your current location and your new home?
- How and when will you move?
- The size of your possessions will help you decide your moving strategy.

SHOULD YOU HIRE MOVERS OR MOVE YOURSELF?

The decision of whether to hire professional movers or move yourself depends on several things, including the size of your move, your budget, and your physical abilities. Because movers typically charge a flat rate based on the distance, it may be cost-savvy if you are moving a longer distance. Even if you think you will save as you will already be making the trip yourself, if you have more items, it will require multiple trips, which will add up the costs.

✚ Pros of Hiring Movers

Professionalism and Efficiency

Experienced movers have the expertise and equipment to pack, transport, and protect your belongings efficiently.

Reduced Stress

Hiring movers can significantly reduce the physical and emotional strain that can come with moving, allowing you to focus on settling into your new home.

Insurance Coverage

Professional movers typically offer insurance coverage for your belongings in case of damage or loss.

— Cons of Hiring Movers

Cost

Hiring professional movers can be expensive, especially for large moves or long-distance relocations.

Limited Control

You may have less control over the packing and handling of your belongings, especially if you choose a full-service moving company.

Potential Damage

Even with insurance, there is always a risk of damage to your belongings during a move.

+ Pros of Moving Yourself

Cost Savings

Moving yourself can significantly reduce the cost of your relocation.

Greater Control

You have complete control over the packing, handling, and transportation of your belongings.

Personal Touch

You can take extra care of your belongings and ensure they are packed and transported according to your preferences.

— *Cons of Moving Yourself*

Physical Strain

Moving yourself can be physically demanding, especially if you have a large move or heavy items.

Time Commitment

Moving yourself requires a significant amount of time and effort, which may be challenging if you have other commitments.

Risk of Injury

Improper lifting or moving techniques can lead to injuries.

Create a Moving Timeline and Schedule

A well-structured timeline and schedule can help you stay organized and avoid last-minute stress. While you can create your own schedule that fits your plans, you can use the suggested timeline and checklist below and adjust it as you wish.

Six to Eight Weeks Before the Move

- Research moving companies or arrange for self-transportation.
- Gather packing supplies and start sorting your belongings.

- Notify utilities and other service providers like banks, insurance companies, the post office, and your employer of your move.
- Change your address with the relevant institutions.

Two to Four Weeks Before the Move

- Pack nonessential items that you won't need to use prior to moving.
- Complete change of address paperwork.
- Schedule movers or arrange transportation.

One to Two Weeks Before the Move

- Pack essential items in separate, clearly marked boxes.
- Deep clean your current home.
- Defrost and clean your refrigerator and freezer.
- Arrange for childcare or pet care on moving day.
- Set up the main utilities in your new home prior to moving so that you do not stress about lights or cold water on your first night there.

Moving Day

- Supervise movers or carefully load your belongings if you are moving yourself.
- Keep important documents and valuables with you.
- Clean up any remaining items at your old home.

After the Move

- Unpack your belongings and arrange the furniture in your new home.
- Reconnect the rest of the utilities and services, such as cable TV and the internet.
- Update your address with any remaining institutions.

Sort Your Stuff Before Packing

Sorting your belongings before packing is crucial for an organized and efficient move. Divide your belongings into categories like clothes, kitchenware, books, and electronics. Identify items you no longer need or use and consider donating them to charity.

Packing Supplies

Gather a variety of packing supplies to ensure your belongings are protected during transport.

Essential items include

- sturdy cardboard boxes in various sizes
- packing paper for wrapping fragile items and filling empty spaces
- bubble wrap for extra protection of delicate items
- packing tape to securely seal boxes and protect furniture corners
- markers for clearly labeling boxes with their contents and destination room to avoid fishing for things that you immediately need after moving

MOVING TIPS FOR A SMOOTH TRANSITION

Proper planning can help make your relocation a smooth transition. You can use the time to go through your stuff and get rid of any clutter to reduce your load and keep only the things you frequently use. Having an organized folder can make things easier as you structure your move accordingly. The following tips will help you have stress-free exercise to move into your new home, making the journey more exciting.

Declutter

Take advantage of your moving and use it to get rid of everything you no longer use. You can sell usable items online or at a garage sale. You can also donate to charity. Leaving only the things you frequently use will make your move smoother and less stressful.

Organize a Moving Folder

If you like digital filing, you can make a folder of all your moving essentials, such as the new address, purchase agreement, payment papers, and moving contracts. You can also make a hard copy to avoid any disappointments should the file get corrupted or your devices go off on moving day.

Pack as Early as Possible

While packing and organizing your moving stuff depends on your schedule and the size of your possessions, it is important to start as early as possible to avoid last-minute stress and chaos. Some people start packing as far in advance as a few months prior to moving, while others prefer to start a month or a couple of weeks earlier.

Book Your Moving Team Early

If you will be using moving services, professional painters, or hiring a truck, you want to secure your bookings as early as possible. Booking late can come with high costs and disappointments. You may not be able to find the team or services you want, especially if you move during peak season when demand is high.

Keep the Essentials Close By

Do not make the mistake of packing everything into the moving truck. Keep the essentials, like your toothbrush, deodorant, toilet roll, pajamas, phone chargers, paperwork, first aid kit, kids' favorite toys, snacks, bottled water, medication, and keys to the new house, with you in the car that you will be using. You might be separated from the moving truck or arrive at different times, so you do not want to encounter any stress because your essentials are stuck in the truck.

Use a Truck With a Loading Ramp

If you are using moving services, you do not have to worry because they come in ready for heavy lifting. However, if you are hiring a truck to move yourself, then do not cut costs by getting a truck without a loading ramp. Avoid straining your muscles, damaging your furniture, or spending a lot of time trying to move heavy furniture yourself. It is not worth it.

Invest in Equipment

You must get all your packing supplies ready. Essentials like moving boxes, tying ropes, adhesive tapes, garbage bags, and permanent markers are a must for smooth packing and moving. You can still use these supplies the next time you move or at your new home.

Use the Right Box Sizes

Avoid piling up things in big boxes to make a few loads. Instead, put items in the correct box sizes so that they are light enough to carry.

Fill Up Any Empty Spaces

Use packing paper, towels, bubble wrap, or foam to fill up any empty spaces in the boxes. Avoid leaving any items loose or moving in the boxes, as it can cause inconveniences and irritation during moving.

Pack Heavy Boxes First

Start with heavier items, put them in the bottom boxes, and pack them first to balance the truck. Pack the lighter items last and put them on top.

Avoid Mixing Items From Different Rooms

Use separate boxes to pack items accordingly. Avoid mixing items from different rooms in one box to avoid chaos and frustration when you need something upon arriving at the new home. Label each box with the room it is destined for. You can even make things easier by labeling each single item inside the box to facilitate unpacking. Individually wrap kitchen utensils before bundling them in boxes. Place dishes on their sides, not flat. Pack your clothes in suitcases or boxes, or leave them in the dresser if they are not too heavy. Separate folded clothes from those on hangers.

Pack Fragile Items With Care

Things like expensive art or TV require extra care when moving. Take care to pack them with as much care as possible to avoid damage. Double the boxes where possible and put them last in the moving truck so that they are not squashed as it moves. If you can, it would even be better to move them separately from the rest of the furniture.

Tape Your Boxes Well

Boxes should be securely closed with adhesive tape to prevent them from opening during moving. Wrap the boxes all around with the tape and double up where you have heavier boxes.

Order Takeout

You will likely be too tired and anxious from the move, so reduce your stress and order takeout instead of worrying yourself about cooking.

Rest

After all the hard work and the long journey, freshen up and rest. You will worry the following day about everything else. Enjoy your first night in your new home.

Finally, Unpack

After a good night's rest, you can start unpacking and organizing your stuff accordingly. Not only will you avoid living out of boxes, but you will settle faster once everything is in its rightful place.

SETTING UP UTILITIES

When moving into a new home, it is crucial to set up essential utilities to ensure you have access to electricity, water, sanitation, and other services. As I mentioned above, it is advisable to set up utilities weeks before moving into your new home so that you have the essentials ready upon moving. You can always set up additional utilities once you have already moved in. The pricing of utilities usually varies by state; what you pay in Hawaii is likely to be three times what someone pays in Louisiana.

Essential Utilities

Electricity

As we all know, electricity is what makes our modern day lights, appliances, and electronics work so don't forget to contact your local electricity provider to establish an account and schedule the connection of electricity to your new home.

Natural Gas

If your home uses natural gas for heating, cooking, or water heating, contact the local natural gas provider to set up an account and connect the service.

Water and Sewer

Contact your local water and sewer authority to establish an account and activate service at your new address.

Trash and Recycling Pickup

Arrange for trash and recycling pickup services with your local waste management company. This ensures the proper disposal of household waste and recyclables.

Additional Utilities

Cable and Internet

If you want cable television and internet access, contact your preferred cable and internet providers to establish an account and schedule installation at your new home. Choosing the right internet service provider (ISP) is crucial for ensuring a fast, reliable, and enjoyable online experience. Below are some tips for choosing the best provider:

- Determine your internet usage patterns, including the number of devices connected simultaneously, the types of activities you engage in online (streaming, gaming, or video conferencing), and your desired download and upload speeds.
- Verify which ISPs offer service in your area and compare their coverage maps to ensure you have access to the speeds you need. Be mindful of potential limitations in rural or remote areas.
- Carefully review the different internet plans offered by each ISP, considering factors like speed tiers, data caps, monthly fees, equipment rental costs, and any promotional offers or discounts.
- Explore online reviews and testimonials from existing customers to gain insights into the ISP's performance, customer service, and overall satisfaction levels.
- Research the ISP's reputation for reliability, uptime, and outage history. A consistent and dependable connection is essential for uninterrupted online activities.
- Read the fine print of service agreements to identify any hidden fees, termination penalties, or contract duration restrictions that could impact your overall costs.
- Consider bundling your internet service with other services like cable TV or phone plans from the same provider to potentially save on costs.
- Ask friends, family, or neighbors who live in your area for their recommendations and experiences with different ISPs. Their personal insights can be valuable.

- Reach out to potential ISPs directly to inquire about their plans, pricing, and any specific questions you may have. Their representatives can provide detailed information and address your concerns.
- Think about your future internet usage needs and choose an ISP that can accommodate potential growth or changes in your online activities.

Home Security

If you are interested in a home security system, contact reputable home security companies to explore options, obtain quotes, and schedule installation.

How to Set Up Utilities

Determine Who Provides to Your Area

If you're new to the area where your new home is located, your real estate agent will have handy a list of utility providers. Or, you can contact your local municipality or property management office to identify the utility providers for your area. They can provide specific information on each provider's contact details, services offered, and pricing.

Contact Utility Companies

Once you have identified the utility provider you need, contact each company to establish an account in your name. Provide them with your new address, move-in date, and any necessary account information. If you are keeping the same provider, you can contact them to help you transfer to a new address.

End the Old Services

If you are going to use a different provider, you will no longer need your current provider. Most utility companies prefer to be contacted 2 weeks before you move out. Therefore, cut ties with the old provider as soon as you have set up the new accounts for the new home. Tell your current service provider the exact move-out date so that they can stop the services.

Check Utility Status

Verify that utilities have been turned off at your old residence and turned on at your new address. You don't want to spend a few days in your new home without lights, water, and heat or cooling.

Timeline of Setting Up Utilities

The timeline of turning off and turning on utilities is important. You don't want to be paying utilities at the place you just left and you don't want to try to move in to your new home before utilities are turned on. If you're moving within the same utility district, you should be able to coordinate with them a smooth transfer of the stop of utilities and the start of utilities in your new home.

Two Weeks Before Move-in

Start researching and contacting utility providers to gather information and start the account setup.

One Week Before Move-in

Confirm account details, schedule service connections, and finalize arrangements with each provider.

Move-in Day

Verify that all essential utilities are functioning properly and address any last-minute issues.

Two Weeks After Move-in

Review billing statements and ensure you are enrolled in the appropriate service plans and pricing tiers.

CONNECT WITH YOUR NEW NEIGHBORHOOD

Connecting with your new neighborhood is how you will feel at home as you become a part of the community. While leaving old friends and neighbors can be tough, you can make things easier by getting to know new people as soon as you settle into your new home. Make it easy for your new neighbors to connect with you by being approachable. Be the first one to smile and say hello so that the awkwardness of being new and out of place is broken and your neighbors will be put at ease with your friendliness.

Tips for Getting Involved:

Mingle With the Locals

Find out about the local activities and events that bring your neighborhood together, such as community gatherings, local festivals, or volunteer opportunities and join in. Your children will make friends easier and feel like they fit in as they interact with other children at local ball games, and community festivities. Immerse yourself in the local culture and interests to find common ground with your neighbors.

Be the First One to Greet

Take the initiative to introduce yourself to your neighbors. Strike up conversations when you encounter them in common areas, such as the mailbox, park, or elevator. A friendly smile and a warm greeting can go a long way toward breaking the ice.

Accept Invitations

If your neighbors extend invitations to neighborhood events or gatherings, graciously accept and attend. These gatherings provide excellent opportunities to connect with others, share stories, and build relationships.

BUYING YOUR FIRST HOME | 199

Be the Host

Host your own neighborhood gatherings or events, such as a potluck dinner, a backyard barbecue, or a movie night. Invite your neighbors to participate and create a welcoming atmosphere for everyone.

Become an Active Community Member

Get involved in local organizations, clubs, or initiatives that align with your interests. Volunteering for community projects or participating in recreational activities can introduce you to like-minded neighbors and strengthen your ties to the community.

Start Networking

Attend local networking events, join business groups, or participate in professional organizations to expand your social circle and connect with neighbors who share your professional interests.

Take Your Dog for a Walk

Walking your dog in the neighborhood is a great way to meet other pet owners and strike up conversations. Sharing a love for animals can be a natural icebreaker and lead to new friendships.

Join an Activity Class

Enrolling in classes at a local college or community center can introduce you to neighbors who share your interests in learning, fitness, or personal development. These classes provide opportunities for interaction and potential friendships.

MAINTAINING AND IMPROVING YOUR NEW HOME

You may have bought your house when it was in pristine condition, but that does not mean that you can relax and go years before any issues arise. Maintaining and improving your new home is an ongoing process that makes sure your investment remains in good condition and continues to meet your needs and preferences. It is also more affordable to do regular maintenance than to wait for serious issues to arise as they will require more money and effort to fix.

Establish a Regular Maintenance Schedule

Create a schedule for routine maintenance tasks, such as cleaning gutters, checking smoke detectors, changing air filters, and inspecting for potential leaks or hazards. Consistency in maintenance prevents minor issues from becoming major problems.

Address Repairs Promptly

Don't let small repairs linger. Attend to them as soon as they arise to prevent further damage or escalation of the issue. Early intervention often saves time, money, and stress.

Deep Clean Regularly

Schedule deep cleaning sessions periodically to thoroughly clean all areas of your home, including hard-to-reach spots and often-overlooked areas. This ensures a healthy and hygienic living environment.

Maintain Outdoor Spaces

Regularly care for your lawn, garden, and landscaping. Mowing, weeding, watering, and fertilizing ensure your outdoor areas remain attractive and inviting.

Protect Your Home from the Elements

Take measures to protect your home from damage caused by weather conditions. Ensure proper drainage, inspect roofs and gutters for leaks, and trim trees away from power lines.

Boost Energy Efficiency

Use energy-saving measures to reduce your utility bills and environmental impact. Consider upgrading appliances, installing· smart thermostats, and utilizing natural lighting whenever possible.

Upgrade and Renovate as Needed

Consider upgrades and renovations that enhance the functionality, comfort, visual appeal, and the atmosphere of your home. Prioritize projects that align with your budget and lifestyle.

SEASONAL TASKS AND BUDGETING

It is important to note that your home will need different care in different seasons. Be sure to schedule relevant maintenance in line with the seasons. You may need to regularly check gutters for leaves in the fall more than you need to during the summer. Anyone whose HVAC breaks down in the hottest summer months will tell you it would have been smart to have their unit checked and maintenance done before the weather got hot. Also, the cost of maintaining your home will vary seasonally, requiring you to have a comprehensive yet flexible budget in place.

Spring

- Clean gutters and downspouts to remove any debris that has accumulated over the winter to prevent water damage.
- Inspect your roof, windows, and doors for any leaks that may have developed during the cold months.
- Keep trees and bushes trimmed to prevent damage from falling branches.
- Clean and repair your lawn mower, grill, and other outdoor equipment, and get them ready for the season.
- Give your lawn a boost with some fertilizer to help it green up.

Summer

- Ensure that your lawn gets enough water to stay healthy during the hot summer months.
- Mulch around your plants to help retain moisture and prevent weeds from growing.
- Keep an eye out for pests like mosquitoes and ants, and take steps to control them if necessary.
- Heavy summer rains can clog gutters and downspouts, so it's a good idea to clean your gutters and downspouts again in the middle of the summer.
- Ensure that your air conditioning unit is working properly to keep you cool during the summer heat.

Autumn

- Rake leaves to prevent them from clogging your gutters and downspouts.
- Apply a winterizer to your lawn to help it survive the cold winter months.
- Drain your outdoor pipes before the weather gets too cold to prevent them from freezing.
- Clean and store your lawn mower, grill, and other outdoor equipment before the winter arrives.
- Seal up any cracks or openings around your home to prevent drafts from entering your home during the winter.

Winter

- Keep your sidewalks and driveways clear of snow to prevent falls.
- If you have any pipes that are exposed to the elements, check them regularly for signs of freezing.
- Dry winter air can damage your woodwork and furniture. Use a humidifier to add moisture to the air.
- Open windows and doors for a few minutes each day to allow fresh air to circulate.
- Make sure your furnace is working properly to keep you warm during the winter.

Budgeting for Repair Costs

Budgeting for maintenance, repairs, or improvements to your home depends on various factors. The common rule of thumb is to have at least 1%–4% of the home's total value set aside for repairs. That would mean putting aside $5,500–$22,000 for a $550,000 home a year, which can be incredibly hard for most first-time homeowners. Factors such as the age of the home, materials used, and climate also play a role in determining repair costs. Some experts recommend that homeowners save at least 5% of their income for repairs and about $10,000 for emergency repairs (Weston, 2022).

Deciding how much you want to spend on repairs will also depend on the lifespan of your appliances or the frequency with which the material used needs to be replaced. For instance, if it would cost $5,000 to replace an air conditioning system that typically lasts 15–20 years, you may want to save $500 every year for it. Having a home inspection every now and then will also save you from seeing problems when they have already exacerbated and need more money.

Another way you can prepare for home repair costs is to access your equity through a line of credit. As long as you make on-time payments on your home equity credit line, you can rest assured that whenever your home repair bills exceed your budget, you have them covered.

Alternatively, you can buy an annual home warranty, which covers most appliance repairs and replacements at an annual fee plus a service fee when a technician comes to do repairs. It can be relatively more affordable than putting aside a percentage of your home's value for repairs.

I think you'll agree, this has been an eye-opening journey full of ebbs and flows. Congratulations once again for staying the course to the finish line. You did it!

Action Steps

❑ Get ready to move by planning your moving schedule: make a timeline for your move with important dates.

❑ Organize your stuff as your stuff as you sort your belongings: Decide what to keep, donate, or throw away.

❑ Get packing supplies: gather boxes, tape, and packing materials.

❑ Start packing early: Begin packing your things early and label boxes clearly.

❑ Choose how to move by hiring movers or doing it yourself. If hiring, book movers in advance, well ahead of time.

❑ Arrange for all utilities to be activated; Settle into your new home

❑ Connect with your new Community: Make friends, join local activities, and be part of your new neighborhood.

❑ Keep your home well-maintained: Create a schedule for repairs, cleaning, and outdoor care.

This includes budgeting for seasonal home tasks: Plan your budget for different seasonal maintenance and repairs.

Next is a summary of what you learned in the book. I suggest you book mark the Conclusion page as a go-to whenever you need a quick refresher on the process of buying your first home.

You can find definitions in the glossary section for the real estate and finance world technical jargon.

MAKE A DIFFERENCE WITH YOUR HOME BUYING REVIEW

UNLOCK THE JOURNEY OF FINDING YOUR DREAM HOME

Buying Your First Home by V J Dean is a must-read for anyone stepping into the world of real estate. With a friendly and approachable style, V J Dean offers practical advice to make the daunting task of purchasing your first home a more manageable and informed journey.

Why Your Review Matters

Your insights and experiences are invaluable! By sharing your thoughts on *Buying Your First Home*, you help others navigate their own home-buying journey. Your review can provide guidance, reassurance, and the confidence others need to make informed decisions.

Writing Your Review: A Simple Guide

We love hearing your thoughts! When writing your review, consider the following:

✓ **Clarity and Honesty:** Be clear about what you loved and what you think could be improved.

Examples: Did a particular piece of advice stand out? Share how it impacted your home-buying process.

✓ **Recommendations:** Would you recommend this book to others? Who do you think would benefit most from reading it?

Remember: Your Words Have Impact

Just like how V J Dean advises not to let emotions override financial decisions in home buying, your balanced and thoughtful review can guide others towards making wise choices. Your words can be the beacon that lights the path for many first-time homebuyers.

Share Your Review Now

Ready to share your thoughts? Just scan the **QR CODE** below to submit your review.

To access the book, type this link into Google, then scroll to the bottom of the page to leave your review: https://a.co/d/4aOeilM

Your generosity in sharing your experience can make a significant difference in someone else's journey to buying their first home.

Thank you for contributing to our community of readers and future homeowners!

CONCLUSION

You will agree with me that homebuying is not for the faint-hearted. It takes effort and commitment to learn the process and navigate through this journey. I am extremely proud of you for making it this far in the book. Making this homebuying journey as a first-timer can be intimidating; however, you can eliminate some of the stress. You've taken the first steps by understanding the benefits and challenges of buying a home, assessing your financial and emotional readiness, and exploring the pros and cons of renting versus buying.

As you dug deeper into the homebuying process, you've also discovered the importance of budgeting effectively, understanding the real estate market, and positioning yourself for better deals. Remember, getting a preapproval is crucial, as it showcases your financial stability and credit ability to potential sellers. Plus, on the quest for a place that reflects your aspirations and lifestyle, knowing your must-haves and flexible features will guide you toward the perfect property. House hunting until you find your dream home requires working closely with experienced real estate agents to secure the deal.

Making an offer is a strategic step that requires careful consideration of market conditions. Whether you're in a buyer's or seller's market, your offer should demonstrate your seriousness and willingness to negotiate. The final step is the closing process, where your homebuying journey is wrapped up and you're handed the keys to that dream home. It is crucial to engage professional help to ensure a smooth and stress-free closing experience. Remember, closing costs are an essential part of the process, and you may have opportunities to negotiate them with the seller.

After this final hurdle, you are now ready to step into your new home, a place where you can create memories and build a lasting legacy. I hope you found Buying Your First Home a great guide to a successful journey.

As a review, following are some of the key takeaways from the book.

Key Takeaways

- Homeownership is a significant financial decision, so it's crucial to assess your financial readiness.
- Understanding the real estate market will help you make informed decisions about buying and selling.
- Being in a position for better deals involves getting preapproved and understanding market trends.
- Knowing your must-haves and flexible features will guide you toward your dream home.
- Navigating the house-hunting process requires patience, persistence, and a willingness to negotiate.

- It's important to seek professional guidance.

As you travel through your homebuying journey, remember that this book has been your trusted companion, providing you with valuable insights and guidance. Please consider leaving a review on Amazon to share your experience with other aspiring homeowners.

I wish you the best of luck in finding your dream home and achieving the satisfaction of true homeownership. Happy house-hunting!

EXCLUSIVE OFFER!

As a small token of my appreciation, here is a Free Gift that will be crucial for your success with this book:

Success Tools for Your New House Hunt: *Free PDF*

This necessary tool is a must as you evaluate and compare amenities when looking at prospective new homes. With it you'll be able to list and detail desired amenities based on your unique desires and needs. It will not only help prioritize what matters most but will also aid in making informed decisions. This focused tool simplifies the comparison of different properties, allowing you to identify the one that best suits your lifestyle and ensures that you can fully enjoy your new home.

CLICK HERE TO GET IT NOW
www.vjdeanpublications.com

GLOSSARY

Adjustable-Rate Mortgage (ARM): A type of mortgage where the interest rate can change over time, making monthly payments more unpredictable, but also offering lower initial interest rates than fixed-rate mortgages.

Amortization: The process of gradually paying down a debt over time. Amortization schedules show how much of each payment goes toward principal and interest.

Appraisal: An estimate of the fair market value of a property.

Credit Line: A revolving line of credit that can be used to borrow money up to a certain limit. Credit lines typically have variable interest rates and monthly payments.

Credit Score: A numerical representation of a person's creditworthiness.

Debt-To-Income Ratio (DTI): A measure of a person's debt obligations relative to their income.

Delinquency: A failure to make payments on a debt when they are due. Delinquency can damage a person's credit score and make it difficult to obtain future loans.

Earnest Money: A deposit of money made by a buyer to show their intent to purchase a property. Earnest money is typically held in escrow and returned to the buyer if the sale does not go through.

Encumbrance: A legal claim against a property that restricts its ownership or use. Common encumbrances include liens, easements, and covenants.

Equity: The difference between the value of a property and the amount of debt owed on it.

Equity Loan: A type of loan that allows homeowners to borrow against the equity in their homes.

Equity Release: A process of accessing the equity in a property without having to sell it. Equity release options include equity loans, bridge loans, reverse mortgages, and home equity lines of credit (HELOCs).

Escrow: An account held by a neutral third party to hold funds and documents until certain conditions are met.

Lien: A legal claim against a property that gives the creditor the right to seize the property if the debt is not repaid. Common liens include tax liens, mortgage liens, and mechanic's liens.

Loan-To-Value (LTV) Ratio: A measure of the amount of a loan relative to the value of the property being financed.

Mortgage Insurance Premium (MIP): A type of insurance required for certain mortgages that protects the lender in case the borrower defaults on the loan.

Preapproval: A preliminary approval from a lender that indicates the borrower's eligibility for a mortgage up to a certain amount.

Prequalification: An initial assessment of a borrower's creditworthiness and ability to obtain a mortgage.

Private Mortgage Insurance (PMI): A type of insurance that is required for conventional mortgages where the down payment is lower than 20%.

Suburbanization: The movement of people from urban areas to less densely populated suburban areas.

Urbanization: The movement of people from rural areas to urban areas.

Zoning Regulations: Local laws that regulate the use of land and the types of buildings that can be constructed in different areas.

REFERENCES

A new homeowner's guide: How to set up utilities when buying a house. (2019, February 14). Liberty Moving & Storage. https://www.libertymoving.com/a-new-home owners-guide-how-to-set-up-utilities-when-buying-a-house/

Araj, V. (2021, March 10). *12 steps to buying a house: A how-to guide.* Quicken Loans. https://www.quickenloans.com/learn/steps-to-buying-a-house

Araj, V. (2023, April 13). *What credit score do you need to buy a house?* Rocket Mortgage. https://www.rocketmortgage.com/learn/what-credit-score-is-needed-to-buy-a-house

Attardo, P. (2019, November 28). *11 reasons you need a real estate agent to buy a home, despite the internet.* HomeLight. https://www.homelight.com/blog/buyer-why-use-a-real-estate-agent/

Bahney, A. (2022, November 3). *First-time homebuyers are being shut out of the market like never before.* CNN Business. https://edition.cnn.com/2022/11/03/homes/first-time-homebuyers-hit-record-low-nar-report/index.html

Bennette, J. (2023, August 8). *The ultimate maintenance checklist to keep your home in top shape year-round.* Better Homes & Gardens. https://www.bhg.com/home-improvement/advice/home-maintenance-checklist/

Bermudez, R. (2023, April 13). *Home inspection vs. appraisal: What's the difference?* LendingTree. https://www.lendingtree.com/home/mortgage/home-appraisal-vs-home-inspection-whats-the-difference/

BHG The Masiello Group. (2019, May 6). *6 tips to get acquainted with your new neighborhood.* Better Homes and Gardens Real Estate. https://www.masiello.com/news-and-updates/2019/05/02/6-tips-to-get-acquainted-with-your-new-neighborhood-2

Bigger house or smaller mortgage? What's best when buying a new home. (2019, February 10). Lifetise. https://lifetise.com/bigger-house-smaller-mortgage/

Bortz, D. (2022, August 11). *10 crucial questions to ask a real estate agent before you hire them.* Realtor.com®. https://www.realtor.com/advice/buy/questions-to-ask-a-real-estate-agent/

Budget to buy your first home. (2023, August 16). RCS Group. https://rcs.co.za/media/budget-to-buy-your-first-home/

The Builders at Wealth Factory. (2022, August 1). *Everything you need to know to make a budget spreadsheet.* Wealth Factory. https://wealthfactory.com/articles/how-do-i-make-a-budget-spreadsheet/

Bundrick, H. M. (2016, May 15). *Why it's important to understand your market during a housing search.* Christian Science Monitor. https://www. csmonitor.com/Business/Saving-Money/2016/0515/Why-it-s-important-to-understand-your-market-during-a-housing-search

Casey, B. (2022, January 31). *9 tips to overcome buyer's remorse for enormous purchases like a house.* HomeLight. https://www.homelight.com/blog/buyer-how-to-over come-buyers-remorse/

Ceizyk, D. (2023, May 2). *Here are 10 benefits of owning a home.* LendingTree. https://www.lendingtree.com/home/mortgage/benefits-of-owning-

CFI Team. (n.d.). *Housing expense ratio.* Corporate Finance Institute. https://corpo ratefinanceinstitute.com/resources/commercial-lending/housing-expense-ratio/

Chen, J. (2023, June 30). *Earnest money: What is it and how much is it in real estate?* Investopedia. https://www.investopedia.com/terms/e/earnest-money.asp

Cho, J. (2019, August 13). *What finally owning a home means to me....* Oh Joy. https:// ohjoy.com/my_weblog/2019/08/what-finally-owning-a-home-means-to-me.html

Crace, M. (2023, March 23). *The ideal credit score to buy a house in 2023.* Quicken Loans. https://www.quickenloans.com/learn/credit-score-to-buy-a-house

Dehan, A. (2023a, June 9). *Escrow fees? What they cost and who pays them.* Rocket Mortgage. https://www.rocketmortgage.com/learn/escrow-fees

Dehan, A. (2023b, July 21). *A guide to the housing expense ratio.* Rocket Mortgage. https://www.rocketmortgage.com/learn/housing-expense-ratio

Dehan, A. (2023c, November 6). *5 types of mortgage loans for homebuyers.* Bankrate. https://www.bankrate.com/mortgages/types-of-mortgages/

Dulcio, B. (2023, August 17). *How to increase your credit score.* Debt.org. https:// www.debt.org/credit/improving-your-score/

Erickson, B. (2022, January 6). *10 home inspection findings you shouldn't ignore.* Equity Trust. https://www.trustetc.com/blog/home-inspection-red-flags/

Finding your property. (n.d.). Just Landed. https://www.justlanded.com/ english/United-States/USA-Guide/Property/Finding-your-property

First-time home buyer budget worksheet. (n.d.). The Summit Federal Credit Union. https://www.summitfcu.org/first-time-homebuyer/first-time-home-buyer-budget-worksheet/

FirstTimeHomeBuyer. (2023, August). *What did you compromise on when buying your first home?* Reddit. https://www.reddit.com/r/FirstTimeHomeBuyer/ comments/15lk4op/what_did_you_compromise_on_when_buying_your_ first/?rdt=56761

Fitzsimons, J. (2022, March 28). *House equity: What is it and why does it matter?*

NerdWallet. https://www.nerdwallet.com/uk/mortgages/what-is-house-equity/

Flyhomes. (2023, May 18). *9 important features to consider when buying a house.* Flyhomes Lounge. https://www.flyhomes.com/blog/features-for-your-new-home/

Fontinelle, A. (2023, March 31). *First-time homebuyer's guide.* Investopedia. https://www.investopedia.com/updates/first-time-home-buyer/

Franklin, J. B. (2022, July 25). *Renting vs. buying a home: Which is right for you?* Bankrate. https://www.bankrate.com/real-estate/renting-vs-buying-a-home/

Franklin, J. B., & Beck, R. H. (2022, September 21). *How to make an offer on a house.* Bankrate. https://www.bankrate.com/real-estate/how-to-make-an-offer-on-house/

Fuscaldo, D. (2022, June 14). *How to set a budget for buying your first home.* Investopedia. https://www.investopedia.com/personal-finance/how-set-budget-your-first-home/

Gerhardt, N. (2023, September 27). *10 things you need to know about searching for homes online.* Family Handyman. https://www.familyhandyman.com/list/things-you-need-to-know-about-searching-for-homes-online/

Gervis, Z. (2018, August 6). *Buying a home is an anxiety-inducing nightmare: Study* New York Post. https://nypost.com/2018/08/06/buying-a-home-is-an-anxiety-inducing-nightmare-study/

Getler, T. (2023, November 22). *Mortgage interest rates forecast.* NerdWallet. https://www.nerdwallet.com/article/mortgages/mortgage-interest-rates-forecast

Giorlando, M. (2023, June 19). *Where should I live? 12 important factors to consider.* Rocket Mortgage. https://www.rocketmortgage.com/learn/where-should-i-live

Gobel, R. (2022, March 9). *Are you ready to buy a house?* Investopedia. https://www.investopedia.com/articles/mortgages-real-estate/10/ready-to-buy-house.asp

Green, D. (2023, November 6). *How to get pre-approved for a mortgage in 4 simple steps.* Homebuyer. https://homebuyer.com/learn/mortgage-pre-approval

Hansen, S. (2022, March 21). *10 cities where homebuyers are most likely to face bidding wars.* Money. https://money.com/cities-with-most-bidding-wars-homes/

Heidenry, M. (2016, December 13). *Top 10 benefits of buying a home: Do you know them all?* Realtor.com®. https://www.realtor.com/advice/buy/benefits-of-buying-a-home/

Highlights from the profile of home buyers and sellers. (2018). National Association of Realtors. https://www.nar.realtor/research-and-statistics/research-reports/highlights-from-the-profile-of-home-buyers-and-sellers

Holslin, P. (2023, October 3). *How to choose an internet provider.* HighSpeedInternet.

https://www.highspeedinternet.com/resources/choosing-an-internet-service-provider

Home buyers wants and needs checklist. (n.d.). Eaton Realty. https://www.eatonrealty.com/blog/buying/home-buyers-wants-and-needs-checklist

The Homeward Team. (2022, March 31). *Four common types of homebuying contingencies.* Homeward. https://www.homeward.com/blog/4-common-types-of-home-buying-contingencies

How to use a mortgage calculator. (n.d.). Chase. https://www.chase.com/personal/mortgage/education/financing-a-home/how-to-use-mortgage-calculator

Investopedia Staff. (2023, May 18). *Conventional mortgage or loan.* Investopedia. https://www.investopedia.com/terms/c/conventionalmortgage.asp

Irby, L. (2022, February 27). *Complete checklist of documents needed for a mortgage.* The Balance. https://www.thebalancemoney.com/complete-checklist-of-documents-needed-for-a-mortgage-5216291

Kalra, R. (2019, April 7). *10 ways to get acquainted with your new neighbors.* Mover Junction. https://www.moverjunction.com/moving-guides/10-ways-to-get-acquainted-with-your-new-neighbors

Kielar, H. (2021, December 13). *Top 11 things to look for when buying a house.* Quicken Loans. https://www.quickenloans.com/learn/things-look-shopping-next-home

Kielar, H. (2023, August 4). *5 types of home loans for all home buyers.* Rocket Mortgage. https://www.rocketmortgage.com/learn/types-of-mortgages

Kilroy, A. (2023, November 11). *A guide to home inspection costs in 2023.* Rocket Mortgage. https://www.rocketmortgage.com/learn/home-inspection-cost

Kuo, J. (2023, June 9). *7 documents you need when applying for a home loan.* Credit Karma. https://www.creditkarma.com/home-loans/i/home-loan-documents

Lake, R. (2021, July 12). *Grab your budget planner and learn how to use it to track spending.* The Balance. https://www.thebalancemoney.com/how-to-fill-out-a-budget-planner-sheet-4777126

Lake, R. (2023, May 6). *Want a better credit score? Here's how to get it.* Investopedia. https://www.investopedia.com/how-to-improve-your-credit-score-4590097

Lewis, H. (2023, November 16). *Mortgage interest rates forecast.* NerdWallet. https://www.nerdwallet.com/article/mortgages/mortgage-interest-rates-forecast

Loudenback, T., & Tarpley, L. G. (2022, August 12). *How mortgage interest is calculated: Formula for monthly principal and tips for figuring out the simple math for your total repayment.* Business Insider. https://www.businessinsider.com/personal-finance/how-to-calculate-mortgage-payment?r=US&IR=T

Luna, K. (2022, August 23). *What are the most common home repair costs?* SoFi. https://www.sofi.com/learn/content/most-common-home-repair-costs/

Marquand, B. (2023, September 28). *How to find the right real estate agent for you.* NerdWallet. https://www.nerdwallet.com/article/mortgages/are-all-real-estate-agents-the-same-which-realtor-is-right-for-you

Marquand, B., & Getler, T. (2023, June 27). *Guide to VA home loans: How they work and who qualifies.* NerdWallet. https://www.nerdwallet.com/article/mortgages/va-home-loan

MasterClass. (2022, January 13). *How to negotiate a house price: 7 negotiating tips.* https://www.masterclass.com/articles/how-to-negotiate-house-price-explained

McWhinney, J. (2023, July 24). *Fixed-rate vs. adjustable-rate mortgages: What's the difference?* Investopedia. https://www.investopedia.com/mortgage/mortgage-rates/fixed-versus-adjustable-rate/

Melore, C. (2022, August 13). *What is a mortgage? Just 49% of Americans actually know, survey shows.* Study Finds. https://studyfinds.org/what-is-a-mortgage/

Mint. (2020, August 25). *10 ways to fine tune your personal budget before buying a house.* MintLife. https://mint.intuit.com/blog/budgeting/budgeting-before-buying-a-house/

Mint. (2022, May 20). *Free monthly budget templates [Simple & detailed template options].* MintLife. https://mint.intuit.com/blog/budgeting/free-budget-tracking-template/

Morris, G. (2022, February 22). *Glossary of terms.* InCharge Debt Solutions. https://www.incharge.org/housing/homebuyer-education/homeownership-guide/glossary-of-terms/

Morris, G. (2023, September 21). *Responsibilities of a new homeowner.* InCharge Debt Solutions. https://www.incharge.org/housing/homebuyer-education/homeownership-guide/responsibilities-of-a-new-homeowner/

Mortgage calculator – estimate monthly mortgage payment. (n.d.). Realtor.com®. https://www.realtor.com/mortgage/tools/mortgage-calculator/

Mueller, L. (2022, April 5). *How to set up utilities in your new home.* Moving.com. https://www.moving.com/tips/how-to-set-up-utilities-in-your-new-home/

Mulvey, K. (2023, January 15). *Should you renovate your home all at once or in pieces?* Real Simple. https://www.realsimple.com/home-organizing/home-improvement/renovations/renovation-remodeling-process

Mutikani, L. (2023, October 19). *US existing home sales drop to 13-year low in September.* Reuters. https://www.reuters.com/markets/us/us-existing-home-sales-drop-13-year-low-september-2023-10-19/

Nearly half of Americans dissatisfied with their homes since COVID-19 hit. (2020, October 23).

BryanRealtors. https://bryanrealtors.com/nearly-half-of-americans-dissatisfied-with-their-homes-since-covid-19-hit/

Neidel, C., & Bundrick, H. M. (2023, September 6). *5 free budgeting templates and Excel spreadsheets.* NerdWallet. https://www.nerdwallet.com/article/finance/free-budget-spreadsheets-templates

Neighbors Bank. (2023). *2023 USDA loan income limit eligibility and county lookup.* https://www.neighborsbank.com/usda-loans/income-limits

Nguyen, J. (2021, December 5). *4 key factors that drive the real estate market.* Investopedia. https://www.investopedia.com/articles/mortages-real-estate/11/factors-affecting-real-estate-market.asp

O'Shea, B., & Barroso, A. (2023, October 24). *How to improve credit fast.* NerdWallet. https://www.nerdwallet.com/article/finance/raise-credit-score-fast

Oboza, A. (2023, March 3). *Coping with emotions during the homebuying process.* Lansing State Journal. https://www.lansingstatejournal.com/story/market place/real-estate/2022/03/03/coping-emotions-during-homebuying-process/9358511002/

Phillips, L., & Milbrand, L. (2023, March 30). *18 moving tips and packing advice for your best move yet.* Real Simple. https://www.realsimple.com/home-organiz ing/organizing/moving/moving-packing-tips

Philps, R. (2023, February 6). *Pre-approved loan offer: What does it mean?* NerdWallet. https://www.nerdwallet.com/uk/loans/personal-loans/what-is-a-pre-approved-loan/

Porter, K. (2023, July 7). *Complete checklist of documents needed for a mortgage.* US News. https://money.usnews.com/loans/mortgages/articles/complete-check list-of-documents-needed-for-a-mortgage

Porter, K., & Jennings, C. (2023, February 10). *Should you buy a bigger house? How to make the right choice.* Credible. https://www.credible.com/blog/mortgages/should-i-buy-a-bigger-house/

Premela, R. (2021, February 5). *20 famous real estate investing quotes.* America Mortgages. https://www.americamortgages.com/20-famous-real-estate-invest ing-quotes/

Rafter, D. (2022, June 7). *Home-buying checklist: Beginner's guide.* Quicken Loans. https://www.quickenloans.com/learn/home-buying-checklist

Rajdutta, A. (2016, May 18). *5 reasons you should hire an expert advisor when buying your dream home.* Makaan. https://www.makaan.com/iq/buy-sell-move-prop erty/5-reasons-you-should-hire-an-expert-advisor-when-buying-your-dream-home

Renting vs. owning. (n.d.). Better Money Habits. https://bettermoneyhabits.banko famerica.com/en/home-ownership/renting-owning-house

Rohde, J. (2022, August 3). *How to do a real estate market analysis like a pro.* Roofstock. https://learn.roofstock.com/blog/real-estate-market-analysis

Roughley, T. G. (2022, October 18). *U.S. news & world report new homebuyer worries survey 2022.* US News. https://www.usnews.com/insurance/homeowners-insurance/new-home-buyer-survey

Ryan, K.-A. (2021, August 12). *The pros and cons of using professional movers.* Mid-West Moving & Storage. https://www.midwestmoving.com/2021/08/12/the-pros-and-cons-of-using-professional-movers/

Rylander, S. (2022, April 18). *9 reasons buying a house will be 100% worth it.* HomeLight. https://www.homelight.com/blog/buyer-is-buying-a-house-worth-it/

Sabella, M. (2022, April 15). *How to organize, plan and prepare for a household move.* The Spruce. https://www.thespruce.com/organize-plan-prepare-household-move-2436542

Santarelli, M. (2023, November 2). *Housing market forecast 2024 & 2025: Predictions for next 5 years.* Norada Real Estate Investments. https://www.noradarealestate.com/blog/housing-market-forecast-for-next-5-years/

Scott, H. (2016, November 7). *10 responsibilities to expect as a homeowner.* The Daily Positive. https://www.thedailypositive.com/10-responsibilities-expect-homeowner/

Segal, T. (2023, September 29). *Federal Housing Administration (FHA) loan: Definition, requirements, limits, and how to qualify.* Investopedia. https://www.investopedia.com/terms/f/fhaloan.asp

Seth, S. (2021, December 9). *13 steps of a real estate closing.* Investopedia. https://www.investopedia.com/articles/mortgages-real-estate/10/closing-home-process.asp

7 reasons to own a home. (2022, July 28). Realtor Magazine. https://www.nar.realtor/magazine/tools/client-education/handouts-for-buyers/7-reasons-to-own-a-home

75 moving tips for a smooth move in 2019 (step-by-step). (2019). ByStored. https://www.bystored.com/guides/75-moving-tips-for-a-smooth-move-in-2019

Shepard, E. (2022, February 16). *7 free spreadsheets to help you budget for buying a house.* Tiller. https://www.tillerhq.com/7-free-spreadsheets-to-help-you-plan-and-budget-for-buying-a-house/

Stieg, C. (2020, October 27). *The psychology of buying a house: Is it a key to happiness or just a source of stress?* CNBC. https://www.cnbc.com/2020/10/27/does-buying-a-home-make-you-happier-psychology-of-home-ownership.html

Sue Ostler Buyers Agent. (2022, November 15). *The psychology of buying a home: Understanding what makes it so stressful.* LinkedIn. https://www.linkedin.com/

pulse/psychology-buying-home-understanding-what-makes-so-stressful-ostler?trk=pulse-article

Team HomeServe. (2022, October 29). *Here's how much common home repairs cost — and how to budget for them.* HomeServe. https://www.homeserve.com/en-us/blog/cost-guide/home-repair-costs/

Torres, K. (2017, August 10). *10 factors to consider when determining the safety of your neighborhood.* SafeWise. https://www.safewise.com/blog/factors-to-consider-when-determining-the-safety-of-your-neighborhood/

Treece, K. (2023, October 12). *Mortgage calculator: Estimate your monthly house payments.* Forbes Advisor. https://www.forbes.com/advisor/mortgages/mortgage-calculator/

TrueBlog. (2020, December 1). *Tips for maintaining your new home.* True Homes. https://www.truehomesusa.com/blog/tips-for-maintaining-your-new-home/

Two smart homebuying moves: Mortgage prequalification and preapproval. (n.d.). Bank of America. https://www.bankofamerica.com/mortgage/learn/mortgage-prequalification/

Union Plus Mortgage Team. (2016, September 5). *How important is it to have a budget when buying a home?* Union Plus. https://www.unionplus.org/blog/consumer-tips/how-important-it-have-budget-when-buying-home

USDA loan income limit eligibility for 2023. (2023, July 13). USDA Loans. https://www.usdaloans.com/articles/usda-income-limits/

Villegas, F. (2021, October 11). *Real estate market analysis: What it is & how to do it.* QuestionPro. https://www.questionpro.com/blog/real-estate-market-analysis/

Warden, P. (2022, April 5). *Home inspection checklist: What to expect on inspection day.* The Mortgage Reports. https://themortgagereports.com/37715/home-inspection-checklist-what-to-expect-on-inspection-day

Waterworth, K. (2023, May 19). *How to choose a home.* US News. https://realestate.usnews.com/real-estate/articles/how-to-choose-a-home

Wells, L., & Beck, R. H. (2023, May 11). *Should you buy a house? 8 signs you're ready.* Bankrate. https://www.bankrate.com/real-estate/should-i-buy-house/

Weston, L. (2022, July 28). *How to budget realistically for home repairs.* NerdWallet. https://www.nerdwallet.com/article/finance/how-to-budget-realistically-for-home-repairs

What are the closing costs for a home loan? (2023, September 30). Sarkari Info. https://info.sarkarigo.com/what-are-the-closing-costs-for-a-home-loan/

What is equity release and how does it work? (n.d.). OneFamily. https://www.onefamily.com/equity-release/what-is-equity-release/

Whyte, S. (2023, October 13). *How much does a real estate lawyer cost?* Clever.

https://listwithclever.com/real-estate-blog/realtor-or-real-estate-lawyer-which-is-cheaper/

Wichter, Z. (2022, January 10). *This seasonal home maintenance checklist will keep your house in shape.* Bankrate. https://www.bankrate.com/real-estate/seasonal-home-maintenance-checklist/

IMAGE REFERENCES

Aguilar, L. (2020, December 6). *Man lawyer office* [Image]. Pixabay. https://pixabay.com/photos/man-lawyer-office-desk-computer-5806013/

Bryant, J. (2018, July 14). *Assorted color wall paint house* [Image]. Pexels. https://www.pexels.com/photo/assorted-color-wall-paint-house-photo-1370704/

Danilevich, O. (2020, September 25). *Black calculator besides coins and notebook* [Image]. Pexels. https://www.pexels.com/photo/black-calculator-beside-coins-and-notebook-5466785/

Danilyuk, P. (2021, May 15). *People shaking their hands in close deal contract* [Image]. Pexels. https://www.pexels.com/photo/people-shaking-their-hands-in-close-deal-business-contract-8112180/

Darmel, A. (2021, April 14). *Real estate agent showing property to a couple* [Image]. Pexels. https://www.pexels.com/photo/real-estate-agent-showing-property-to-a-couple-7641856/

Hassan, M. (2018, March 8). *Financial planning report* [Image]. Pixabay. https://pixabay.com/photos/financial-planning-report-chart-3207895/

Higgins, R. (2017, August 25). *Confused hands up* [Image]. Pixabay. https://pixabay.com/photos/confused-hands-up-unsure-perplexed-2681507/

Ikwuegbu, E. (2021, May 8). *An electrician repairing a fuse box* [Image]. Pexels. https://www.pexels.com/photo/an-electrician-repairing-a-fuse-box-7861963/

Kindel Media. (2021a, April 8). *Man and woman standing besides an agent* [Image]. Pexels. https://www.pexels.com/photo/man-and-woman-standing-beside-an-agent-7578905/

Kindel Media. (2021b, April 8). *Person holding a keychain with key* [Image]. Pexels. https://www.pexels.com/photo/person-holding-a-keychain-with-key-7578984/

Miroshnichenko, T. (2020, September 15). *Recruiter interviewing a candidate* [Image]. Pexels. https://www.pexels.com/photo/recruiter-interviewing-a-candidate-5439438/

Neumann, J. (2019, October 8). *The search for a house* [Image]. Pixabay. https://pixabay.com/photos/the-search-for-a-house-property-4532392/

Piacquadio, A. (2018, September 8). *Focused architect drawing on paper in the studio* [Image]. Pexels. https://www.pexels.com/photo/focused-architect-drawing-on-paper-in-studio-3760532/

Pidvalnyi, O. (2021, October 12). *Real estate homeownership* [Image]. Pixabay. https://pixabay.com/photos/real-estate-homeownership-homebuying-6688945/

Pixabay. (2012, June 23). *Grey metal case of hundred dollar bills* [Image]. Pexels. https://www.pexels.com/photo/grey-metal-case-of-hundred-dollar-bills-164652/

RDNE Stock Project. (2021a, May 28). *A close-up shot of an agent pointing rates with a ball point pen* [Image]. Pexels. https://www.pexels.com/photo/a-close-up-shot-of-an-agent-pointing-rates-with-a-ballpen-8292880/

RDNE Stock Project. (2021b, May 28). *A man in safety vest and hard hat checking the front door* [Image]. Pexels. https://www.pexels.com/photo/a-man-in-safety-vest-and-hard-hat-checking-the-front-door-8293673/

RDNE Stock Project. (2021c, May 28). *Real estate agent giving a printed document to a buyer* [Image]. Pexels. https://www.pexels.com/photo/real-estate-agent-giving-a-printed-document-to-a-buyer-8292793/

Stanly8853. (2017, November 18). *Cottage trees path* [Image]. Pixabay. https://pixabay.com/photos/cottage-trees-path-trail-house-2955582/

Starflames. (2010, May 7). *People joy smile* [Image]. Pixabay. https://pixabay.com/photos/people-joy-smile-holiday-friends-2295052/

0Subiyanto, K. (2020, April 19). *Multiethnic couple packing ceramic belongings in parchment before relocation* [Image]. Pexels. https://www.pexels.com/photo/multiethnic-couple-packing-ceramic-belongings-in-parchment-before-relocation-4246193/

Vasquez, R. (2017, September 23). *Red and white children playing road signage* [Image]. Pexels. https://www.pexels.com/photo/red-and-white-children-playing-road-signage-592600/

Made in United States
Cleveland, OH
30 December 2024

12779798R00125